Hippie at Heart Self-Help Series

DROP THE
Drama!

How to get along with everybody, all the time

MARGARET NASH

Contents

Introduction

"We are biologically programmed to find other human beings the most important objects in the world. Because they can make life either very interesting and fulfilling or utterly miserable, how we manage relationships with them makes an enormous difference to our happiness."

Mihaly Csikszentmihalyi—*Flow*

This book is about how to get along with everybody, all the time, no matter who you are, no matter how cantankerous, and despite any past relationship disasters. I don't care if you just got in a fight with the bank clerk, nearly caused a road rage disaster, or just egregiously offended your best friend of forty years. You can change. We all can.

You absolutely can learn how to get along famously with everyone you come in contact with. But you may need to make some changes in your behavior. You may need to drop the drama. Now.

So my advice is to read this book cover to cover and put your nose to the grindstone practicing the skills and techniques offered

1

here, until you get the hang of them. It will be worth your while.

According to the Stanford Research Institute, 85% of your success is related to people skills—communication and rapport skills— and only 15% to technical skill and ability.

That's pretty startling to me. 85% is really high. That means people skills are way more important than any other skill or talent.

I know we can think of some obvious exceptions, like Steve Jobs of Apple Computers, who was notorious for his abrasive communication style but nevertheless hugely successful.

But in general it would seem that getting along with people is a high stakes game. The success of every part of your life—finances, friendships, who you live with, your career and work, and even your health—to a great extent (85%?) hinges on how well you interact with people. Get it wrong and nothing much will work for you; get it right and everything will flow smoothly.

You can be prosperous, have a great career, be highly intelligent, gorgeous, and talented—but if you cannot get along with people, it will be all for naught. You won't be happy nor have peace of mind.

If you can learn how to adroitly manage your relationships, it can mean the difference between having good friends you enjoy, a tribe where you feel welcome, supportive personal partnerships, and a satisfying social life—or being caught up in drama, ruffled feathers, and feeling isolated and annoyed with everyone. Take your pick. The choice is really is up to you and not your genetics.

Anything is Possible!

I promise it's possible to get along with everyone you come in contact with, even if you were born with a contrarian, rebel temperament like I was. This book will chronicle how someone *not naturally* sweet or even tempered (moi), quick to anger, slow to calm, whose automatic reaction in most situations is to speak first and think later, has garnered the secrets of damping down her natural instincts and learning to behave. My parents and school couldn't control me; I had to learn the hard way.

Believe me it's been worth it. Life is so much easier now that I'm able to keep my mouth shut at appropriate times, maintain calm in the face of provocation, and keep my cool when I feel like lashing out. Hey, most of the time. Nobody's perfect.

All That Counts

What counts is how we behave towards others. Full stop. It's not about what we are thinking or feeling, what story we are telling ourselves about someone, or the kind of person we think we are. *It's what we say and do and how we say and do it* that will determine how well we get along with everyone.

And that means we have to let go of over-reaction, hurt feelings, getting offended, and being touchy and awkward with people.

The good news is you can get different results in your life if you're not happy with what you're getting now, and are willing to do *whatever it takes to change.*

You're going to need some determination and absolute conviction that you're going to make this work. Most relationships take effort to bloom and flourish, and require a deeply inspired motivation and belief that the effort is worth it.

In this book I share with you **six drama-draining social skills** for managing all your relationships, and I guarantee you they work. Always. And once you learn these skills, and put them in practice, you can relax and enjoy life without worrying about making peace with the latest person you've upset. Everything will go better for

3

you— friendships, family, work colleagues, partners, ex-partners; all will run smoothly and seemingly effortlessly.

Does that sound appealing? *If only*, I hear you cry?

This book is about getting it right. It's about nipping drama in the bud before it takes over and spoils everything.

A Simple Purchase

Way back in 1996 I made a simple purchase that changed my life. It's one of those times when you can identify a decision that altered the course of your destiny. These decisions are called 'choice points' and invariably made rather casually, and when we look back we breathe a sigh of relief, accompanied by a slight sense of panic, that we went ahead and carried them through. *What if I hadn't... turned that corner, spoke to that person, picked up that book? Given him my phone number?*

So let me share. I was living in England at the time, an American by birth, enjoying a successful career as a sales and management trainer for a high tech company in Britain. In the interests of improving my training skills I decided to attend a one-day course in stress management, near Heathrow Airport, on the outskirts of London. As a trainer it was win-win; I could glean what content the trainer had to offer and pick up some tips on presenting to a large group of people. It also involved a pleasant day out where I could watch someone else perform, without the stress, and pretend it was in the interests of work.

That day turned out to be pivotal in my life—incredibly useful and eye opening. The trainer inspired me and kept the group enthralled with stress management the entire day, no small feat, and became a role model for me. I was in awe of her skills and wanted to learn as much as I could.

But it was the purchase I made in the back of the room, at the end of the day, that really turned my world around. Destiny calling!

When the training ended I wended my way up through the crowd to speak with her, curious if she had any advice to help me along with my fledgling career. Her recommendations were sound if slightly predictable—become expert in my subject and read and study everything there was available. OK, I can do that. Then she added, *"You must buy this tape set I'm selling. You'll love it. It will help you more than anything else to get you started on the path."*

I was sold in a flash. The tape set was Brian Tracy's, *The Psychology of Achievement.* I bought it, listened to it, devoured it; I had never heard anything like it before. I listened to it in my car, and in my kitchen while cooking; I took it to bed with me. I memorized it.

It was the beginning of a brand new and exciting era for me, a time in which I became fascinated and obsessed with personal development, self-help, and the whole human potential shebang. It inspired me to take courses and gain certificates in NLP (Neurolinguistic Programming), Hypnosis, Life Coaching, and Time-line Therapy, and sent me off happily on a completely new, and some might say, wacky, path in life. Boy, was it fun.

But most of all, it gave me the secret of learning how to get along with people. All people. All the time, if I so chose. Brian Tracy had *The Secret.*

San Miguel de Allende—A Little Piece of Paradise in Mexico

A little background. I am writing this on the veranda of my home in the town of San Miguel de Allende, a beautiful colonial haven in the central highlands of Mexico. It is the end of January and the weather is glorious—clear blue skies, a soft breeze, and bright winter sunshine.

My dog is napping peacefully beside me on the sofa, and my cat has found the only spot of sunshine on the veranda and is lazily rolling around and stretching in ecstasy. There are hummingbirds and orioles in the trees, and two doves are fooling around noisily on a branch close by. And of course I'm working hard. Indeed.

San Miguel is a cozy town of very human dimensions— everything is within walking distance, no building is over three stories high, and when you venture into town you always meet up with someone you know, whether you want to or not. There are over 10,000 foreigners living here, attracted to the climate, the culture, the color, the art and Spanish colleges, and the friendly welcome from the Mexicans.

We foreigners, mostly from the States and Canada, are here to make a new life for ourselves and are eager to make friends, socialize, drink Margaritas, and eat tacos. It's easy to connect with people and that is something I appreciate after living in England for three decades. I love England, but it can be a little reserved. I have some good friends here and I value these friends all the more because it wasn't always this way for me.

Let me tell you my heartbreaking tale. Get the tissues out.

A Preacher's Kid Leaves Home and Discovers the Big World

I grew up in the Deep South, in Alabama, a preacher's kid, and from an early age I was aware that I wasn't especially easy to get along with. I come from a line of Germans and Scots and tend to be rather direct and opinionated about…well, just about everything.

I was the baby in a family of five, and definitely a bit spoiled. My two older sisters teased me a lot— I'm sure because they could easily make me burst into hysterical fits of anger—which brought them endless entertainment. Temper tantrum was my middle name.

An early Drama Queen.

In school I wasn't *un*popular, but I always *felt* like an outsider. That was my perception of things. I was extrovert and could be funny, but never *felt* part of the in-crowd. I was also a little moody and this increased my sense of being hard to get along with.

My high school yearbook listed no activities under my name. None whatsoever. I simply had zero interest in groups and school activities, being in the band, or sports. Needless to say, I was never cheerleader or prom queen. So yes, you could say I was a bit of a misfit.

It was my belief that I was a maverick, a bit different, and I felt perpetually on the outside looking in, an outlier. I suspect a lot of people feel this way growing up, and our stories about ourselves have a way of proving themselves true. Our brains filter in evidence to validate our beliefs.

At age eighteen I left home to go to what was quaintly referred to back then as a 'girls' school', in Atlanta, Georgia. That term carried a lot of connotations. It was a Presbyterian college for upper class, mostly rich, mostly very conservative, young Southern ladies. I certainly didn't fit in with that crowd; the only thing I had in common was I was female, young, and Southern. The perfect set up for me to feel even more isolated than in high school.

I gathered more evidence of my weirdness. The story grew and expanded.

Graduation and England!

As college graduation approached, the opportunity to do summer volunteer work in England came up and I was off in a flash. My first 'choice point'! I make decisions impulsively, and I didn't give it a lot of thought. I just knew the moment I saw the flyer saying,

7

"Would you like to do social work in England this summer?" that I would go. Yes indeed, the *Adventuress* in me had awakened, never to sleep again.

The Hippie Movement and England

Let me backtrack a little. While still in college in the late 1960s, the youth counter-culture movement burst upon the world, and I embraced everything about it with alacrity. It fit me to a tee. Suddenly it was OK to be different, to have radical ideas, to be a rebel. In fact, it was cool. For the first time I had found my tribe— hippies! Rebellious, weird, non-conformist, outsiders all.

So this was the state I was in when I saw the poster about social work in England. I was ripe for an adventure and England was the place to be—the birthplace of hippiedom. I took off to England in the early 70s on my social work jaunt and it was all terribly exciting and fabulous. It was the land of the Beatles, after all, and London, Carnaby Street, double-decker buses, and young men with long hair wearing ruffles and velvet. How fab was that? The accents thrilled me, *so* Beatles, *so* Mick Jagger. I determined to stay forever and set about making this happen.

I was still an outsider, mind, albeit now with an excuse—I was a foreigner, a 'bloody yank'—and I didn't mind that so much. Being loud and intense fit in with my American image. It gave me a sense of identity.

And there in *ye olde countrie* I met my first husband, a graduate from Cambridge University: erudite, well spoken, complete with English accent (fancy that), and a total, genuine hippie, whatever that meant. Longhaired, poetry reading, politically savvy—he seemed to be the real deal, not one of those pretenders from Georgia Tech or Emory.

8

I ended up staying for over twenty-five years.

We quickly got married, settled down, and became 'normal', focusing on survival and raising a family. And I still had that old left-out feeling, like I was somehow different from everyone else. I didn't fit in easily with the English 'young mums' set for sure. Just like at college, and high school before that, I didn't quite slot in anywhere.

It's worth noting that I had a fairly quick temper and was prone to drama filled reactions to provocation. I could be difficult sometimes. This was becoming a carefully honed story I created about myself. Trust me, it didn't help.

This feeling of semi-isolation went on for years, even when I had a successful career. Then I discovered Brian Tracy and *Wham! Bam!* I realized I could change this sense of disconnection and not have to feel like the perpetual outsider. I could be *however* and *whoever* I wanted to be; my fate was in my hands. I was determined to change directions...and Brian Tracy was my *ticket to ride*.

My Life Now in Mexico

Years later, after three children, an entirely amicable divorce, and a move back to this side of the Atlantic, I am living in Mexico with my second husband, who is Mexican. The adventure continues.

Since those times long, long ago, a lot has magically transformed for me. I now have more than one circle of good close friends, and I'm part of a few different tribes. People (amazingly) seem to think I'm pretty easy to get along with, at least that's what they say, and I have great relationships with my friends. I get along with all my relatives. I get along with my ex-husband and his wife. I get along with my three grown-up kids who live in England.

I only ever fight with people on Facebook (Ack! I know. I'm not proud of that) but I do know how to keep the peace with those I deal with face to face. I know how to let go of the stories I make up about others and the situations I find myself in. They are rarely true, and never helpful.

I'm not bragging, seriously, because it wasn't easy to get to this point. *And I've done it without changing my basic personality.* I'm still me. I'm still a Rebel, and as they say in England, 'feisty'. I'm an old hippie at heart and I'm pretty intense. It isn't my natural style to be easygoing and *it doesn't have to be yours.*

But things are working for me people wise because now *I have strategies for doing so!* That's the secret and I'm going to reveal the skills involved to unlock that secret.

If I can do this, you can too. That's what this book is about. No matter what type of personality or character you have, you can maintain and manage your relationships in a comfortable way and get along with people. All people. You can feel part of things, and at ease with whom you are.

What counts is how you act and how well you control yourself and your emotions, and for that you simply need to learn certain skills. They are all here, six of them. You can do this.

You Don't Need to Suffer

What is obvious to me from my experiences with friends and life-coaching clients is that many people suffer enormously and unnecessarily because of relationship issues. Most of my clients come to me with problems with the people in their lives—and on any given day are squabbling, getting their feelings hurt, offending others inadvertently, and experiencing stress and unhappiness *due (in their minds) to other people and the stories they make up about them.*

10

I can say unequivocally that these problems cause the most anxiety—even more than health and money issues. And they can *cause* health and money issues. Think about it, if initially that doesn't ring true. Good relationships can tide you through health and money problems; on the other hand, you can have great health and all the money you need, but without good relationships, you are not likely to enjoy any of it.

The premise of this book is that if you just drop certain habits and adopt others, you can have a happier, more successful life. In all areas.

I call this my *drop* and *adopt* strategy. Read on.

The Brilliant Premise

So getting back to my pivotal purchase all those years ago, what was it I discovered in Brian Tracy's *The Psychology of Achievement* that changed my life? (*Still available at www.briantracy.com/catalog/the-psychology-of-achievement. Now on MP3 or CD but not the old tapes I had!*)

His theme, and the presupposition of this book, is that *superb* human relations are within anyone's reach.

Furthermore, you don't have to change your personality or become docile and submissive. You don't have to conform, nor struggle to become easy going. You can be sharp, iconoclastic, radical, and opinionated, and people will still like you as long as you follow a few simple rules. Fancy that.

You can be who you are. I certainly don't want you to change that.

Please take this away if nothing else. Getting along with people is *a set of skills* anyone can learn. You simply need to practice the skills, and follow certain rules. It's never too late to learn them!

Drop That. Adopt This

Here are some of Brian Tracy's teachings:

- Never, ever complain. Nobody likes a complainer. If you complain all the time, people will avoid you. Drop it.

- Never, ever criticize. Nobody likes it and nobody appreciates it. Drop it.

- Never, ever argue. It won't change anyone's mind and you will just cause offense. Drop it.

- Accept everyone. Just let them be. Don't try to change anyone. Adopt this.

- Be excruciatingly patient and polite with everyone. Adopt this. It works.

That's it—Tracy's relationship philosophy in a nutshell. It works for him. He's enormously popular and loved, but he will tell you it wasn't always that way. He had to learn the hard way, like I did and maybe like you do.

All of these points abolish drama. There is story making behind *every single problem* we have with other people.

In this book I expand on this and outline some habits, mind-sets, and attitudes that you need to **drop** right now. And in each chapter I identify a behavior or skill to **adopt** that will counteract the old habit.

Some of them are gleaned from ancient teachings. Some are from my experiences as a Life-Coach, trainer, hypnotherapist, and human being. Many come from Neuro-linguistic Programming (NLP), others from Toltec wisdom, Eckhart Tolle, Joseph Murphy,

Science of Mind, and of course Brian Tracy and scads of others in the personal development world.

The Hippie at Heart

This book is for anyone who needs it, but is dedicated to all you hippies at heart—rebels, free spirits, fiercely independent unconventional types who just want to live life on your terms, without drama or wasting good energy trying to put out fires you have started.

Maybe at heart you are a heretic and never totally fit in comfortably with an orthodox, conventional lifestyle. Or maybe you are a lone wolf and not totally domesticated—a little cranky, cantankerous, and sometimes not easy to get along with?

That's OK! I like people like that! Don't you? People who march to their own drummers aren't always placid and serene.

But for sure, no matter what our disposition, we all want to have friends, keep them, and we'd prefer not to be alone. Deep down we all just want to get along with everyone, be happy, and get by with a little help from our friends.

This book is for you! It will help you, I promise.

Sacred Cow Alert!

In addition in this book I will challenge some Sacred Cows of modern new age thinking and personal development. Somebody has to.

A Sacred Cow is a metaphor for something considered too sacrosanct to question, even when it needs to be.

The term comes from the sacred cows of India, which are allowed to roam freely because of their divine status. These cows will trample your garden, eat your flowers and hold up traffic with impunity.

The Cow will moo about things you can be and do (*You can be whatever you want! Just visualize it!*) but conveniently leaves out the hard work needed to make it happen.

Blessed Bovines

Some of these Cows have gotten out of control and need to be rounded up and sent back to the meadow. Their wise old sayings have become clichéd and can be heard almost everywhere —on the psychologist's couch, from new age evangelical pulpits, in training, in marketing, in books and at seminars. They are political correctness in the personal development world gone wild. Nobody is allowed to question them.

So we're going to shoo some of these cows off your patio where they have taken up residence, lying on your couch and munching your plants, and send them off into the sunset where they belong.

Watch out for **Sacred Cow Alerts!** throughout the book.

A Completely Empowering Mindset

The ideas and skills outlined in this book are empowering and mostly come from NLP, (Neuro-linguistic Programming)—a practical, unorthodox, self-help system of psychological techniques. These techniques are pragmatic and not concerned with theory or dogma; the only questions they ask are:

Is what you're doing working for you?

Is the story you're telling yourself empowering you?

If not, what do you need to change to make it work?

The really cool thing you will discover is that once you change your behavior, your feelings will follow quickly. You start to *feel* relaxed and easier to get along with when you start *acting* as if it were true.

And once you let go of the story, which causes the upset, which then causes the negative emotions, life becomes easier. If you let yourself create drama, then you feel you must justify it and the story will build like a snowball.

This book will teach you how to stop the story in its tracks.

We often get this the wrong way around and think we have to *feel* motivated before we can act. You will discover this is simply not good advice; learn how to behave first and the positive feelings will follow, as you witness how well it works.

The world needs Pirates and Rebels, Cynics, and Curmudgeons. It would be a dull place without them. So join me and discover the first skill for you to adopt. You can start immediately to change your quality of life...

Skill #1
Take 100%
Responsibility for
Whatever Shows
up in Your Life

You mean I have to give up my excuses?

"With everything that has happened to you, you can either feel sorry for yourself or treat what has happened as a gift. Everything is either an opportunity to grow or an obstacle to keep you from growing. You get to choose."

Wayne Dyer

It was southern California, Los Angeles, the summer of 1998. I was in Orange County for NLP training with Tad James— certifying as a trainer in Neuro-linguistic Programming. At the time home was Reading, England, just outside London, so a trip all the way to California was quite an indulgence and I intended to enjoy every moment.

The training lasted for 3 weeks and I lived in a delightful bubble of unreality: studying self-development techniques, practicing them, and discussing intoxicating ideas with exciting new friends late into the night. All without the responsibilities of home and work. Ah, bliss. Guilty pleasure.

Tad, our trainer, had a habit of having lunch with a different group of students every day, giving each of us a chance to ask him questions in private that we may not have wanted to share with the whole group. I was excited when it was my day—I had an important question about someone in my life who was causing me a lot of stress, and I wanted some sage advice from Tad the Oracle.

That day after lunch we went outside the hotel to hold our question and answer session while lounging on the lawn. We wanted to enjoy the southern California weather, which has to be experienced to be believed—warm, sunny, breezy—blissful perfection in weather. We were all full of anticipation.

"Margaret, what is your question?" Tad asked. I launched into some detail about the problem I was having with a troublesome person in my life and how it was impacting so negatively on my peace of mind.

I waited for his wisdom, like a dog for a treat.

Instead of answering me the way I expected, he simply put his open palm right up in front of my nose. *"See that?"* he asked. *"That's a mirror. Whenever there is something going on in your life you don't like, imagine you are holding up a mirror in front of you. Therein lies the problem and therein lies the solution. Nowhere else. Whatever is happening in your life—look in the mirror."*

What?!! That was not the sympathetic, understanding, and bromide filled advice I was craving. No indeed. I wanted to be enabled in my victimhood. I was angry for a moment. Was he saying that I was to *blame* for my problems? That they all came from me?

Tad James was not known for being sweet or accommodating; in fact he had a rather scary reputation for being provocative and uncompromising. He was direct, his advice unsweetened, so I really shouldn't have been surprised at the response I got from him.

"So this is all my fault because I somehow created this? Is that what you are saying? Isn't that blaming the victim?" I bleated, rather defensively.

"No. I'm saying you are responsible for it. Big difference. And until you accept responsibility for what you have created, you will never be able to change it and create something better."

Those words sank into my brain and stayed there, surly and uncompromising, fighting and arguing with my sensitive, touchy ego before finally settling into some sort of acceptance and recognition.

I try to live by them now. They are my go-to mantra whenever something is going on in my life that I don't much like:

"Look in the mirror. Therein lies the problem and therein lies the solution."

I say 'try' because I still have knock-down-drag-out battles with them now and then when I try to pretend I have nothing to do with the results I'm getting in life. Eventually I give in and set about trying to figure out how I manifested the latest mess. Only then do I come up with the solution.

Thank you Tad. I've heard the lesson many times since then, but it was your words that had the most impact on me.

What Tad Was Saying: Take 100% Responsibility for Whatever Shows up in Your Life

You heard me. 100%. Not 50%, not 90%—100%. Even if it's not strictly speaking true, take 100% responsibility. Even if the other person involved turns out to have bad intentions, take 100% responsibility. Even if the other person is blatantly, utterly wrong.

Why? Because that is the *only* way you will avoid being a victim in life. It is the only thing that stands between you and blaming—your parents, your partner, your genes, bad luck, the Universe, God. If you let yourself off the hook even a little, it won't work. It's got to be 100%.

This is such strong medicine! I know! Who wants to think they created the problems they have in life? Remember, this is not about blame, but responsibility. It's actually quite empowering—it implies that if I somehow unwittingly created this mayhem, then I can consciously un-create it and design a more elegant solution. But it's going to take some effort on my part.

(Caveat: Remember, this book is not about abusive relationships.)

Sacred Cow Alert!

The Cow says:
"You have chosen everything that happens in your life."

Wrong! You didn't! Nobody *chooses* to get cancer. Nobody *chooses* for someone they love to die. Nobody *chooses* to be in a car crash. Nobody *chooses* to be born with a birth defect.

You did not choose it because choice requires awareness and conscious thought. Who would consciously choose pain and hardship? As Eckhart Tolle, the spiritual writer and philosopher, says in his book, *The Power of Now,*

"It always looks as if people had a choice, but that is an illusion. As long as your mind with its conditioned patterns runs your life, as long as you are your mind, what choice do you have? None."

And,

"Nobody chooses dysfunction, conflict, pain. Nobody chooses insanity. They happen because there is not enough presence in you to dissolve the past, not enough light to dispel the darkness. You are not fully here. You have not woken up yet. In the meantime, the conditioned mind is running your life."

Tolle goes on to say that choice implies consciousness—a high degree of consciousness. Without it, we have no choices.

So let's round up that Sacred Cow that says we have *chosen* whatever has happened in our lives. That is not the same message as Tad was giving.

This Cow can be really annoying. She makes a lot of noise and is responsible for a lot of guilt and self-blame. If what has happened is negative and painful, we can't consciously have chosen it, unless we are crazy. And if it's unconscious, then it wasn't a choice.

Like all Sacred Cows, there is always some truth in the original. But too often this Cow seems to blame us for all the bad things in our lives, and that's just simply not helpful. This Cow evolved originally from highly esoteric teachings that say we choose everything, even our parents, before we are born. While this is an attractive idea, it's not always *useful* when we are told that this is *why* we are suffering *now*. Especially when we have no memory of why we made the choices. If it was in a former life, then by definition it is unconscious to me now.

Taking responsibility is more helpful than feeling guilty or remorseful about unconscious choices.

We may have *unconsciously created* the situations that show up in our lives, but we didn't necessarily choose them. By accepting responsibility instead, we can then start to understand and become aware of *how* we created things that happen. We can then create something different that works better.

So drop the guilt and the blame—that's not what this skill is about.

Life is Like...a Deck of Cards

Here is a metaphor for life that often helps me if I feel inclined to feel sorry for myself or wallow in victim mode.

Life is a like a *deck of cards* and each of us has been dealt a different hand. You can't change the hand you have been dealt but it is totally up to you how you play that hand.

So you can whine and moan and feel sorry for yourself for whatever hand fate has dealt you, or you can take control and play it the best way you can.

Viktor Frankl, in his thought provoking and groundbreaking book, *Man's Search for Meaning*, which chronicles his experiences in Nazi death camps in World War 2, says that *attitude* is our final bastion of choice. Nobody can force us to change our attitude—not death camps, not pain, not even death. We can always choose how we think and feel about any situation and in that way we are can always be triumphant. "*My smile beneath the tyrant's frown...*" as the old hymn goes.

The Victim—Why Me?

I know (and I'm sure you know) people who are chronically sick or accident-prone. Every time you speak to them, you will be regaled with stories of doctor visits, car accidents, and some new ailment that is totally impacting the ability to get anything done. As soon as one illness is over, something new and even more awful appears.

You instinctively know that they are mysteriously creating the accidents and illnesses. But if you try to confront them and suggest that they are *choosing* these problems, I assure you, *guarantee* you, it will not be received well. They will almost certainly get angry and upset at the very suggestion that they are to blame for their pain and suffering.

Quite right too. That belief is simply not helpful.

When bad things happen to us, most of our pain comes from resisting what is going on right now; we don't like and it and we feel we don't deserve it. And more pain comes from trying to figure out—why me? Instead, if in every situation you can just accept *what is* and take responsibility for what happens next, then life will start to take a welcome turn for the better.

Drop Blame: Adopt Responsibility

So, you are not to blame for that car crash, or the child with a deadly disease. No one is to blame for the hurricane or tornado. You are certainly not to blame if you have been attacked or violated.

But by taking 100% responsibility for what shows up in your life you *can* choose how you respond to it. You can choose to be a victim or victor. *That* part is up to you.

Responsibility creates awareness. Awareness enables choice.

But let's get back to the subject of this book—relationships. How does taking 100% responsibility for my life impact my relationships? Let's explore this more closely.

How's That Working for You?

I'm going to borrow that question from Dr. Phil McGraw of TV fame. It's his signature question and it actually cuts to the chase in every issue. Is what you are doing working, or not? Is it bringing you peace of mind, joy, harmony, and good results? If not, are you willing to do something about it? *How's that working for you?*

Examine your relationships. Are you ok with how you are getting along with your friends and acquaintances? Or…

- are you forever getting your feelings hurt and constantly involved in silly arguments

- you feel bad for being snippy with the clerk in the bank or the waiter in the restaurant

- you are feeling uneasy about that impending family reunion because you had an argument with a cousin last year

- your conscience is bothering you because you snapped at someone, or over-reacted to something somebody said

- you feel embarrassed that you flounced away from the lunch table in a snit over a harmless remark?

How's that working for you?

If it's not, are you willing to change? Take charge of your life? Create a new reality?

Karma! —The Law of Cause and Effect

The belief in the law of karma is old as the hills. It simply means you 'reap what you sow' and that every effect has a cause. All actions are linked together inextricably, and absolutely everything has a cause that originated somewhere.

That traffic accident wasn't random. There were many causes, including the state of mind and emotions of everyone involved, leading up to it.

In many instances it's easy to recognize the cause, with others not so easy. The sick child or any unjust suffering of the innocent is hard to explain. People who believe in reincarnation attribute inexplicable events to actions taken in former lives. Others will say that *God moves in mysterious ways*.

It's not the purview of this book to discuss such deep conundrums. In relationships, it's usually pretty easy to discern the causes of conflict.

My trainer, Tad James, taught that the first task of therapists and coaches is to bring their clients to be 'at cause'. Almost everyone who comes to a coach as a client is 'in effect' and not 'at cause'. In other words, they believe they are victims of circumstance and not in control of their results. The job of the coach is to get them to be at cause, and to recognize they are in charge of what is happening in their lives.

Taking 100% responsibility for your life involves recognizing that everything has a cause and that if you aren't getting along with people, then there is only one place to turn. Look in the mirror. How did you create what you are getting? It may have been unintentional, but bring it out into the light, blinking, snapping, and glaring, and take a hard look at how you originated the problem.

It means you have to STOP blaming other people, circumstances, your parents, your partner, or your hormones for your problems. Stop it! Drop it! There is no compromise here.

Acknowledging your role in your relationships, recognizing that great relationships don't just happen, but are created and nurtured, is behind **Skill # 1**. Adopt it. It is immensely empowering. You *can* change your life. You *can* create a reality that you love.

Make it your mantra.

I take 100% responsibility for what shows up in my life.

A Tale of Two Mornings

I feel somewhat embarrassed to tell this story on myself, but it demonstrates this concept so brilliantly that I feel I must.

One morning I had been on Facebook, wasting time, as one does, and had come across one of those disturbing posts about some injustice that had been perpetrated in another part of the world, on people I don't know, and am pretty powerless to help.

It put me in a cranky mood, but I was unaware of the cause of it. Look what followed…

From Bad to Worse

I left the house to do some errands. On the way out of my neighborhood, someone pulled right in front of me without looking. I honked angrily. *Can't people drive in this country?* (Mexico) It was a neighbor, who glared at me. Oops.

Then, I stopped at the bank. There was a long queue. Usually when I'm waiting in line, I take the opportunity to practice patience, deep breathing, thinking about my goals, or my next book. I try to practice detachment. Or I bring along my Kindle and read. Not today. I sighed deeply and loudly at the inefficiency of this long line.

By the time it was my turn, yes, you guessed it, the interaction didn't go well. The bank clerk was unhelpful. I didn't have the right identification, and she was sorry but she couldn't make the transaction—even though she had seen me many times before. I left with raised eyebrows and an exasperated expression.

Stress Levels Rising.

Next, I visited the dry cleaners. As I explained what I needed done in my broken Spanish to the man behind the counter, I saw in the corner of my eye, two young employees giggling together and glancing over at me. Laughing rudely at my Spanish I suppose! I flounced out in a huff, vowing to myself never to return to that place.

In the Immortal Words of Homer Simpson: Doh!

It was then the penny dropped. I suddenly realized I was creating this bubble of ill will around me and if I didn't stop it now (drop it!) my day was just going to get worse. I saw clearly what I was doing and traced it back to the cause—an unpleasant post on Facebook, which had triggered all sorts of negative emotions in me and put me in a bad mood.

I'm normally patient in the bank. I usually would laugh with those girls who were giggling at me in the cleaners. I would shrug my shoulders and grin. My Spanish *is* funny.

I decided to *drop* the mood and *adopt* my mantras that I usually repeat to myself before going out to interact with the world:

I am calm, confident, in control.

I am unfailingly polite and friendly with everyone I meet.

I repeated them until I took hold of my mood and chilled out. I pulled out and started driving. At the next intersection, I stopped and let a car out. The driver waved and smiled at me in thanks. Ah. That's better! I smiled back. That felt good.

Final stop was the post office. When it was my turn I smiled and apologized for my Spanish. The clerk went out of her way to resolve my situation and get my package sent in the right way.

Back in control! I was now *consciously creating my world* and it was a much friendlier one than before. Taking responsibility. I turned this near disaster of a morning into a good reminder of how easy it is to become unconscious, a victim of the poison around us, and to create results we don't want.

Remember, your emotions dictate your reality. Take control of how you are feeling and never, ever, indulge your bad moods. Drop it. No excuses not even Facebook.

How Did I Create This?

Try this technique from NLP to make sense of an interaction that you are not happy with, or a situation where you feel you are the victim of unreasonable behavior on someone else's part, or a difficult relationship with a friend or acquaintance.

1. Choose an interaction that didn't go well or a situation that was difficult with X. Imagine the other person, X, is sitting opposite you. Choose a word that describes X's behavior.

2. Now imagine that you are X and you are looking at yourself. Look through X's eyes. This is called putting yourself in the other person's shoes. How would X describe you and your behavior?

3. Now imagine you are stepping outside both you and X and are looking at the two of you in the uncomfortable situation. What do you notice? How would you describe what is going on? How are both people creating what is happening?

4. Notice how all relationships are mirrors. What do these two, (you and X), need to do to change this situation? What can you do differently to create a new reality?

5. What was your role in creating X's behavior? Since you can only change yourself, what can you now do to make things work better?

Use this technique for any unpleasant situation or relationship. Use it as a learning tool—it will help you let go of negative emotions or distress around something that happened and you can't change. It will help you do better next time. *What can I learn from this? What can I do better next time? How do I take charge?*

Review

That was **Skill #1** to having great relationships; Take 100% responsibility for whatever shows up in your life. Now let's look at the next skill. What do you think is first cousin to taking responsibility for your results? The next skill may surprise you...

Skill #2
The Meaning of Your Communication is the Response You Get

Did I really say that?

"Depending upon how it is used, the word can set you free, or it can enslave you even more than you know. All the magic you possess is based on your word. Your word is pure magic, and misuse of your word is black magic."

Don Miguel Ruiz—*The Four Agreements*

Following on closely for taking full responsibility for your results is this next skill; *the meaning of your communication is the response you get*. It means what is says—that no matter what you *meant* to communicate, what someone *perceives* is what you sent. Full stop.

The implication is that you have to take 100% responsibility for your communication if you want smooth running relationships.

"Yikes!" I hear you say. *"This surprises me. I can't be responsible for the way people interpret what I say. If they get in a huff, or take it the wrong way, that's not something I need to worry about. It's their problem!"*

Sacred Cow Alert!

The Cow says:
"It's not about you; it's about them.
Don't take anything personally."

This is a really Sacred Cow and I don't intend to kill it, just round it up and bring it in for questioning. *Don't take anything personally* has been a postulate in the world of personal development for years, and many people have taken it to heart as gospel. There is no question many have benefited from it; like all Sacred Cows, it's got legs.

The good intention behind it is that it empowers people to say what they mean and if their words are misinterpreted, to recognize that it is the projection of the other person. This is true.

It also encourages people to place the responsibility for miscommunication on the person who misunderstood. *He took what I said the wrong way. His problem, not mine.* The other person is at fault, not I.

I agree that there is a lot of power in not caring what other people think about what you say or do. It can be liberating and many people can benefit from not caring too much.

In his book *The Four Agreements* Don Miguel Ruiz says we must not take things personally:

"Nothing other people do is because of you. It is because of themselves. All people live in their own dream, in their own mind; they are in a completely different world from the one we live in."

And again he says that in those instances when someone deliberately acts negatively towards you then you mustn't take it in:

"That person tried to send poison to you and if you take it personally, then you take that poison and it becomes yours. Taking things personally makes you easy prey for these predators, the black magicians. They can hook you easily with one little opinion and feed you whatever poison they want, and because you take it personally, you eat it up."

Don Miguel is talking about how important it is to protect yourself against the thoughts, opinions, and negativity that other people wittingly or unwittingly send you. This is Toltec wisdom and of course, good advice. He is also warning against getting offended by what people say about you, which is an excellent habit to adopt.

But…there is more to the story.

What is my beef with this Sacred Cow? Just this. Many people take this to mean that they can simply *ignore* whatever other people think and feel; everything is about the other person and not their problem.

This is not totally true.

How other people respond to you IS your business. It has to be, otherwise if something isn't working how will it get better? How can you take 100% responsibility for your life if you ignore how other people respond to you?

Don and His Dog

Don lives in el Centro of San Miguel de Allende, the lovely colonial town in the highlands of Mexico. San Miguel is a UNESCO World Heritage Site and the central section, El Centro, is a highly sought after area to live for tourists and foreigners.

In El Centro you don't need a car and everything is close to hand; just step out your door onto the cobblestone streets and you will be greeted by a plethora of vendors selling indigenous jewelry and clothes, donkeys, a parade celebrating another saint's day, coffee shops, markets. Your senses will be overwhelmed and many people love living here for just these reasons.

It's also noisy. Mexican towns are not known for their peace and quiet. The apartments are carved out of centuries old buildings and are not well suited for modern life. There is no soundproofing. Dogs are everywhere and they bark a lot. The Mexicans don't seem to notice it, but the barking frequently upsets the foreigners.

Don called me one day. *"My neighbor is insane, evil."* He complained. *"He started playing his drums loudly at 3 am last night and wouldn't stop. I didn't sleep a wink. It was deliberately done to harass me. He wants to drive me away. He hates me for some reason, although I have always been respectful. But you would be proud of me—I am totally sending him peace and love—I know this is all about him and not me. I'm saying my mantras and just ignoring him. He will get his karma."*

"Wait, Don. Is this about your dog and his barking?" I asked, slightly alarmed.

"Well yes. But it's just a dog! This is Mexico! There are dogs everywhere! We have to live and let live!"

Don had a kind heart and had recently rescued a stray dog that had a barking problem. Although Don loved the dog and fed him

33

well, the dog was left alone in his small apartment most days. This particular neighbor had told Don on a number of occasions that the dog barked constantly and seemed distressed at being left alone. Don ignored this and the dog continued barking. He barked at night too if anyone happened to wander by the apartment. He would get hysterical and Don couldn't quiet him.

I could envision the scenario—the dog had been barking again while Don's neighbor was trying to sleep. The neighbor just snapped and decided to enact a little revenge on Don with his drums. Although this was a rather childish response, I couldn't really blame him. Don seemed impervious to how his own actions (and his dog) affected others. This at least got his attention.

Unfortunately, the lesson was lost on Don. Don was an avid student of self-development and especially loved Don Miguel Ruiz with his Toltec wisdom; he frequently quoted from *The Four Agreements* and loved the agreement about not taking things personally. He stood by that teaching and applied it to everything that happened in his life.

But his self-awareness stopped where his personal responsibility should have kicked in. Everything was about the other person and not him. Everything was somebody else's problem and not his.

Don needed to recognize his own role in the nightmare that had been created with his neighbor. He needed to take it personally and find a way to stop his dog barking. It wasn't OK. He was the one being disrespectful, yet he was so lacking in self-awareness that he thought he was the respectful one and the other at fault.

So beware of unconsciousness. *Beware of darkness...*Corral this Sacred Cow that tells you to not take things personally and make sure you hang around its neck the proviso that you also take responsibility for what you say and do.

In other words:

1. Don't take things personally...and...

2. Take everything personally.

Don't take things personally means avoid taking on other people's negativity and world view; it means not getting offended and being overly sensitive; it means avoiding drama and not believing the stories people make up about you. It entails recognizing that every person you come in contact with has a different mindset and model of the world and that their emotions and ideas are about them and not you. So don't take what they say personally.

Take everything personally means that you take responsibility for how your communication comes across to people. If the other person doesn't 'get' your intentions then it is your responsibility to put it right. Learn to be flexible—if what you are doing isn't working, then be willing to try something different. If *you* don't change, nothing will. It's all up to you.

It's all about balance—isn't everything? So be detached from the other person's model of the world and recognize it's not about you...and balance that with taking responsibility for how you come across to other people.

Cleaning up Our Communication—Direct vs. Indirect Communication

Some people are direct communicators and others are indirect. The direct person says what she thinks, clearly and unequivocally; she is not a wilting violet. If you are a direct communicator the advantage is that people will get what you mean, and you have no difficulty stating your needs and intentions.

The disadvantage is that you can sometimes come across as aggressive, hurtful, or insensitive. Too blunt, in other words. Scary.

Being a **direct communicator** means you need to be careful how you are perceived by others and to be willing to soften a bit if you need to. I'm an overly direct communicator and it's one of my challenges.

If you are an **indirect communicator** it means you shy away from telling people exactly what you want them to do or how you are feeling. You think people should 'get the hint' or intuitively understand what you want. This can be a problem if you are with a direct communicator who doesn't take hints and wants you to be specific and clear in stating your needs.

This can cause problems in marriages and intimate relationships.

"Of course you know I love you! I do all these things for you, look after you, pay the bills."

"But you never tell me! How am I supposed to know—read your mind?"

Indirect communicators like to show others what they mean through their actions. The direct communicator wants to be told expressly. This is the cause of many divorces and breakups. Friendships can suffer as well. Feathers get ruffled.

There is no question that direct communication can take a lot of psychic energy sometimes. It's easier just to skirt the issue than confront it. But in the long run avoiding what needs to be said just means the problem keep coming back.

The Solution—Know Thyself

The solution is first to become aware of what sort of communicator you are and what sort the other person is. It's not hard to figure out.

36

Most of us know as soon as we hear the description. And of course sometimes you will be one way and sometimes another. But what is your preference?

Identify your modus operandi and then take responsibility—practice being more direct if you tend to be indirect. Don't assume people are psychic and understand what you mean, even if you think it's obvious.

And if you are direct, recognize that you can sometimes offend or intimidate people. Tone it down, be gentler, and use softer language. Be willing to flex a bit. Stop scaring the socks off people.

Soft Language

Some words are emotionally charged and can evoke strong negative reactions in people. Certain words can sound harsh, especially to an indirect communicator. You may want to be aware of them and use them carefully. These words can put the other person in defensive mode because they imply judgment or criticism.

Some emotionally charged words

- But. (But signals a criticism is following. I don't mean to be disrespectful, but…)

- Ought, ought not. (Judgmental. Drop it.)

- Must, mustn't. (Judgmental)

- Should, shouldn't. (Bossy. Schoolteacher-ish)

- Why? (Confrontational. Forces the other person to defend or justify. Why did you do it like that?)

Soft words

- And…(And sets up expectations for something good)

- May or might. (You may want to think about doing it this way…)

- Can or could. (Sets up possibilities)

- I'm wondering…(Questions gently and non-confrontationally)

- How. (Non-confrontational. Opens up the conversation. I'm curious how you came to that decision.)

Use phrases such as

- I'm sure you will want to…

- I feel certain you will be able to…

- I'm wondering it you have thought of…

- I'm curious as to why…

These are language 'softeners' and will work well with almost everyone. Indirect people especially appreciate kindness and courtesy in their interactions.

Direct people on the other hand, might be impatient with such language. *Spit it out, just get on with it,* or *say what you mean,* are phrases that come to mind with them. They want you to be explicit, no nonsense, and clear. That is what they value. They don't want to pussyfoot around and have to hallucinate in order to understand you. They won't get their feelings hurt if you are say it like it is.

However, when in doubt, always use soft language.

Assertiveness vs. Aggressive or Submissive Behavior

The first cousin to direct communication is assertiveness. Many people mistakenly confuse being assertive with being aggressive. They are not the same.

- **Aggressive** behavior is when I don't take your feelings into account: I state what I mean without being sensitive to how it comes across and whether my words will offend. It can frequently come across as being angry or upset and can include harsh words with no softening phrases.

Aggression is seldom effective and can send signals we are out of control of our emotions.

Sarcasm is aggressive. It is meant to belittle the other.

- **Submissive** behavior on the other hand is when I refuse to express myself clearly for fear of offending. I am so anxious or frightened of negative reactions that I repress all my feelings.

Over apologizing is submissive.

Over explaining yourself is submissive.

Submissive behavior is also ineffective. It is indirect and the other person has to try and figure out what you are feeling. They can figure out wrong and misunderstandings occur. The result of repressing feelings is that they sometimes snap! and become unexpectedly aggressive and angry. They have so many pent up emotions that they just eventually spill out, usually over something silly.

You may know a shy, unassertive person who suddenly is inappropriately angry and attacking. That is the result of being too submissive.

Assertive is the best

- **Assertive** behavior is the best behavior in all circumstances. We express ourselves overtly but without being aggressive or submissive. We say what we feel without anger or emotion; clearly and precisely. We use lots of "I feel" statements but without emotion attached.

"I feel uneasy with what you are saying here. Or, *"I feel uncomfortable with what's going on."*

"I feel" statements are powerful; no one can argue with what you are feeling. They can't reply that you are wrong—you've simply stated your feelings.

Contrast the above statements with; *what you are saying is wrong.* Or—*This behavior is awful.* Each of those sets up resistance and is more apt to start a fight than a dialogue.

When things aren't clear or there has been a misunderstanding, with **assertive** behavior we can use statements such as,

"George, help me here. I'm imagining that you are upset with me since you didn't reply to my emails." Or

"Sandra, I'm sensing you are unhappy with what happened yesterday. Would it be good to talk about it?"

When we are assertive rather than aggressive or submissive, we make it easy for the other person to tell us the truth. George and Sandra can easily reply to those statements. They are not challenging or threatening. When you are assertive you can use humor and be good-natured. It eases up communication, takes the charged emotion out of it, and opens up the channels.

Arguing—A Form of Aggressive Behavior

"...I have come to the conclusion that there is only one way under high heaven to get the best of an argument—and that is to avoid it. Avoid it as you would avoid rattlesnakes and earthquakes."

Dale Carnegie—*How to Win Friends and Influence People*

Brian Tracy tells a wonderful story on himself that took place in the early days of his career. He said that he used to love to debate and argue and that no one could ever win a dispute with him. He was sharp and incisive and always right. However, he had few friends and frequently found himself alone at social events.

Tracy recalls one memorable evening when he was at a party and overheard a discussion starting on a subject he knew a lot about. As he eagerly approached the group in order to jump in and argue his point of view, he saw the people in the group look up, see him coming, and then just fade away and disappear into the crowd. The group completely dispersed and he knew it was because he was coming over. It was then he realized what the problem was; people disliked him because he was trying to be right all the time. He was being a jerk. And nobody relishes being wrong.

That was a turning point for him, a choice point. He decided then and there to stop arguing completely and forever, because it just wasn't working for him. Since then he has been popular and a welcome guest wherever he goes.

Arguing? Drop it. You will never make friends or keep the ones you have if you argue a lot. A big feather ruffler. You never will change anyone's mind and will just build up resentment. We are not talking about informed debate or disinterested discussion, but argument for the sake of proving yourself right.

41

Arguing causes drama. The hidden agenda is we want to get attention and show people how smart we are.

"So figure it out for yourself. Which would you rather have, an academic, theatrical victory or a person's good will? You can seldom have both."

Dale Carnegie—*How To Win Friends and Influence People*

Review

So to recap:

- The meaning of your communication is the response you get.

- You are in charge of your communication, so take control.

- Don't take things personally and take everything personally.

- Clean up your language and way of communicating in order to improve your relationships.

- Learn to be assertive and not aggressive or submissive.

- Stop arguing. Now. Forever.

Let's move on to **Skill# 3**. Are you curious? Let's find out what it is. The next skill is kind of a conundrum, but crucial to keeping the peace. Of all the skills, this next one may save you a lot of unnecessary heartache.

Skill #3
Never Lie: But You Don't Always Have to Tell the Truth

Please don't take this the wrong way, but...

"If you and I want to stir up a resentment tomorrow that may rankle across the decades and endure until death, just let us indulge in a little stinging criticism—no matter how certain we are that it is justified."

Dale Carnegie—*How to Win Friends and Influence People*

What Endures Forever?

Nobody likes criticism. If you want to ruffle a few feathers then there is no better way than with criticism. Few people take it well. Only certain people, who are expert at what they do and sincerely want to get better, welcome criticism. The rest of us resent it and will not thank you for it. Especially unwelcome is unsolicited advice. Unsolicited advice is merely criticism hiding behind the cloak of pretending to be helpful.

"I can't understand why she took it that way. I was just trying to be helpful. Somebody needed to tell her."

Said the person with no friends.

Or how about:

"With all due respect..."

"Please don't take this the wrong way...."

It is one of Brian Tracy's tenets of good relationships—never, ever criticize. Drop it. Non-negotiable.

If you find yourself feeling critical about someone, ask yourself if you are jealous or resentful of that person.

If you are asked for your honest opinion then there are certain ways to handle it without hurting feelings or causing deep-seated resentment.

"When dealing with people, let us remember we are not dealing with creatures of logic. We are dealing with creatures of emotion, creatures bristling with prejudices and motivated by pride and vanity."

Dale Carnegie—*How to Win Friends and Influence People*

Giving good feedback that doesn't offend, or demotivate, is a skill worth learning. Nothing causes hurt more than criticism taken the wrong way.

Brian Tracy says to drop criticism completely from your agenda; however sometimes we are asked our opinion, or we need to critique others for their work. It is crucially important that you know how to give it in an inoffensive way and in a way that will not set up resistance to the message.

Oh dear, I feel a...

Sacred Cow Alert! ˙

The Cow says:
"Always speak your truth!"

There is no argument that truth is important and crucial to good relationships. Be impeccable with your word—one of the Four Agreements alluded to earlier.

Yes, but. The truth can frequently hurt. Speaking the truth should not be an excuse for being insensitive or wounding. You simply don't have that right. Be impeccable with your word, but sometimes it's best to just be quiet and say nothing. You don't always have to speak your truth.

Three 'Play Nice' Questions

Before you do any kind of truth speaking, feedback, or criticism, it's crucially important to ask yourself these three questions:

1. Do I need to say it? (Almost certainly no.)

2. What do I hope to achieve? (What do I want to happen as a result of this? Is there a way for anyone to win out of this or will the result only be destructive?)

3. What is my motive in saying it? (Are my intentions pure or am I looking for revenge or to get back at someone? Am I angry or jealous? Do I have a hidden agenda? Am I just getting something off my chest?)

Asking these questions will save you and everyone else a lot of heartache. Most of the time we are better off just saying nothing when what we are feeling is negative.

When in doubt, keep quiet.

• Think before you speak.

• Don't rise to the bait.

• Don't let someone rattle your cage.

• Don't comment on that dress.

You don't have to express what you are thinking or feeling every moment of the day.

The problem is nobody ever forgets negative criticism. It lasts a lifetime. People everywhere are carrying around hidden away in their subconscious minds negative remarks from their childhood. Stinging remarks on the playground stay with us forever. A disparaging comment from a teacher turns us permanently away from math or science.

Criticism has a way of lodging in the mind like a parasite, sitting there stubbornly, chawing away, and undermining you at unexpected times.

You don't want to be responsible for afflicting someone else in this way. Watch what you say! Your words are more influential than you realize.

Feedback Sandwich—the Most Useful Relationship Technique Ever in the History of the Universe

If you learn nothing else from this book other than how to give non-offensive feedback, it will be worth your while. In my experience, nothing has served me better in getting along well with people than this simple technique—*The Feedback Sandwich.*

You may feel you already know about the *Feedback Sandwich*, and I imagine the term is familiar. I will explain how it works and try to convey why it works so well. Even if you don't get it perfect, it indubitably works better than direct, unfiltered, and un-asked for honesty. It is the ultimate softener and will be extremely useful to you in your relationships.

The name *Feedback Sandwich* is meant as a metaphor for making something palatable; you are making something that is potentially bitter, i.e. advice or suggestions for change, easy to swallow. Bread is easy to digest—if you need to imagine your bread is organic, whole-wheat and gluten-free, fine. Whatever it takes to make your critique digestible.

The *Feedback Sandwich* works with everybody, all the time. I will stand by that over-generalization because it has never let me down. Use it whenever asked to give feedback, every time, without fail. You will be glad you did.

Here's how it works:

The Sandwich

Let's imagine you need to give feedback on an article one of your staff has written. You are the editor, or someone whose role is to comment.

Step #1: First slice of bread

- *Say something nice about the article.* Find something positive to say, even if it wasn't your cup of tea. This places your feedback in context and enables the recipient to receive the rest of what you are going to say. It softens the conscious mind and lowers any resistance to hearing you.

E.G. *"I thought your article was really well written and had a lot of useful information."*

(Context: I liked it. It has a lot of value.)

Step #2: the Sandwich filling—the feedback

The next word you use is crucially important. You have said something positive. If you now say the word *'but'* you will cancel out the nice feeling you have built up. The word *'but'* signals something bad is coming your way. The other person will set up resistance immediately and will cancel out what you are preparing to say, no matter how well intentioned. The drawbridge will be pulled up and the moat impassable.

- Use the word **and** instead of **but**. And sets up anticipation and lowers resistance. Then make your suggestions for change.

E.G. *"**And** I'm wondering if you have thought of adding a section on how specifically it has affected the local community. I think that would significantly increase the impact."*
You can use phrases here such as:

"...and I'm wondering if you have considered..."

"...and what I think would make a difference..."

"...and I imagine you have already thought of..."

"...and I'm curious as to how X would work..."

Step #3: second slice of bread.

- *Finish with a positive statement;* something relevant, the result of implementing the feedback.

E.G. *"I feel this would be an added bit of flavor that would really make this article pop and bring home the message. Well done".*

That's it. That's the *Feedback Sandwich.*

1. Say something nice to give an overall pleasant context

2. Say, and, plus the suggestion for improvement

3. Wrap up with a nice comment.

It works because it recognizes that even the most mature and evolved of us can be sensitive when hearing about our shortcomings. We don't like it. The *Sandwich*, in a way, disguises the flavor of criticism and makes it digestible. It reduces resistance and enables the recipient to receive and understand the advice.

Context is King

A positive context is essential in all our interactions. It doesn't just apply to specific feedback. Think about it—we get along with our friends and intimate partners as long as we feel it is in the context of being loved and valued. Take that context away, and suddenly things start to fall apart. Once we start to doubt that we are cared for and that we matter to the other person, the relationship can become shaky. That is when we take things the wrong way, or get offended by casual remarks.

Context is key to all good communication. Take care to place your communication in a positive context so the other person knows your intention is friendly.

Take responsibility for your communication being **direct, clear, and assertive**. Make sure you aren't being aggressive and pushing someone in a corner where his only choice is to fight his way out.

Ensure your communication isn't submissive i.e. beating around the bush, afraid to say what you mean for fear of being offensive. It doesn't work and just leaves the other person unsure about how you are feeling.

Use the *Feedback Sandwich* with *all* advice or suggestions. What you think of as useful advice can be received as an insult. Never criticize and avoid giving advice if you can. If you must tell someone something about what they have done, then use the *Sandwich* to avoid offense.

Learning How to Deal With Badly Given Criticism

"How people treat you is their karma; how you react is yours."

Wayne Dyer

It would be nice if everyone learned to give elegant feedback that was easy to receive and respond to. Unfortunately you are more likely to be the recipient of badly given criticism than of that

50

thoughtfully given. It can be helpful to learn how to respond when you've been blindsided by a negative remark, and feel like lashing back angrily. How you react is what counts.

In NLP (Neuro-linguistic Programming) there is a technique called the *Learning from Criticism Strategy* that helps you create a useful perspective and give a measured response when taken unawares by a harsh remark or criticism. The technique encourages you to put yourself in the other person's shoes and understand where they are coming from with their remarks.

Learning From Criticism Strategy

When you hear negative remarks coming your way, imagine you are going onto a balcony, and looking down on 'you' and the other person. Notice what dynamic is going on between the two people below you. Watch yourself being criticized.

Going to the balcony gives you distance from your emotions. Just pretend it is the person *down there,* and not you, feeling the distress or anger.

Imagine what the other person's intention was in making the remark. Try and get inside his or her head.

Then choose from the following list of preferred responses. These responses will further defuse the situation and give you more of a chance to gain emotional control so that you don't react angrily.

Preferred responses: choose the most appropriate for the situation:

- **Agree**—they were right! "Thank you for pointing that out to me."

- **Apologize**. *"I'm sorry to have offended you in that way..."* (in this context saying this is not submissive, it's taking control. Say it without anger or sarcasm.)

- **Explain** your perception of the event. "Hmm. What I understood was that this happened..."

- **Ask** what they would have preferred you to do instead. "What would you have preferred that I did in the situation?"

- **Let them know** you prefer not to discuss it at the moment. *"I'm choosing not to comment on that right now."*

(Thanks to Connirae and Steve Andreas)

Learn these responses and rehearse them so that they become automatic. Then you will be able to choose the one in the moment that will get the best results for you. These responses give you back control when you are angry or upset and out of control. Try them— they work beautifully!

OK, But What About Religion and Politics?

If you go on social media, you may be excused for thinking that religion and politics are the cause of all dissension in the world. Many of us find that differences in these two areas are the most difficult to accept in friends and family. Families can be torn apart and friendships discarded due to widely varying opinions and beliefs.

Oh, I know. It's tough to reconcile in these areas, hard to keep your mouth shut, mainly because these opinions are deep seated and usually involve core values. Our political beliefs can reflect our basic attitudes towards how people should be treated and our values around justice, fairness and freedom. I've begun to believe that most of us basically want the same things in society, but our interpretation of how that can be achieved is vastly different. We also differ widely in who we think are responsible for problems in the world.

Our religious beliefs and opinions are basic and core. We usually take on these beliefs at a very young age and because of this they can be hard to shift. There tends to be a lot of fear around challenging these beliefs; it's hard to change an opinion if you believe that you are compromising your soul if you do so.

So is it impossible to get along with people who hold widely or totally different political or religious beliefs?

No. It's easy. I do it all the time. I've always been considered the black sheep of my Alabama family—the weird one who must be going through a phase (50 years and counting). So if I didn't know how to get along with people who hold different beliefs I would be missing out on my wonderful, funny, exciting…and for the most part very conservative family.

My strategy? Simple. Get curious. Be there to listen, to learn. Find out why they think so differently from you. Drop the drama and keep your opinions to yourself—if they are going to start a fight. Stop identifying with your opinions. They aren't you. They are just ideas your ego has gathered and latched onto to create your identity. So are theirs for that matter.

It's fine to have your opinions, but when they get in the way of relationships then you have to make a choice—opinion or relationship. I know which I choose.

Of course I'm not talking about evil opinions another might hold. If someone I'm with, (not my family fortunately) speaks mean, racist, sexist, or homophobic views then I won't choose to keep my mouth shut. I will definitely speak out. But having different political or religious opinions is different. And I'm more tolerant with family. You don't have to have friends who hold vastly different beliefs from you. That's your choice.

Some points for getting along with people of differing political or religious views:

- You've heard the phrase "**Pick your battles**." If you argue and fight over every single area of disagreement, then you dissipate your influence.

- Look for **areas of agreement** and focus on those. Then if you have a core value challenged and you feel you must speak up, your opinion is more likely to be listened to.

- Be aware of your **hot buttons**—those ideas or opinions that really make you unreasonably angry—and be careful and conscious of them. They can get you in a lot of trouble.

- **Walk away** if you have to avoid a fight that will not change anyone's mind and may spoil a relationship. If it makes you that angry, you may have other issues involved you are unaware of.

If you find you are fighting a lot over political or religious ideas, then stop and ask yourself if you are identifying too strongly with your opinion. If you are, then drop it. It's not worth it. It's not you. Let it go and detach from it. You can still support the issues involved, but fighting over ideas is never smart and rarely changes anyone's mind.

Drop it. Remember the Inquisition from the Middle Ages, where thousands were killed and tortured over religious opinions and ideas that we don't even think are important today; it wasn't a good thing. Sorry to say it's still going on today, in the supposedly enlightened 21st century. Don't engage in your own mini-inquisitions!

Review

Well, that was **Skill #3**—never lie; but you don't always need to speak your truth. Frequently it's better to just be quiet. Learn how to give good feedback and how to take criticism without getting upset. This gives you power and self-control in all your interactions.

Please practice the techniques offered here; they are the keys to harmony and peace of mind. You will be admired for your elegant way of handling things!

Onward and upward to the next **Skill**. This next on is something some people seem to be born with and others have to learn. Politicians win elections with it and celebrities cultivate it. But the point is, it CAN be learned. Find out how…

Skill #4
Rapport—the Secret Skill of Many Successful People: (Exception: Computer Geeks)

What do Taylor Swift, Ronald Reagan, and Bill Clinton have in common?

"A rigid building will collapse in an earthquake while a building with built-in flexibility in the foundation will survive the quake."

Robert Dilts

DROP THE DRAMA!

A Tale of Two Blondes

The other evening I was lazily channel surfing on TV when my attention was drawn to a program where Taylor Swift, the young and very successful country singer, was giving a concert. I stopped to watch out of curiosity; even though her music is not written for my age group, I knew about her from the media. She had burst onto the music scene a few years previously and had won numerous Grammys and other music awards. Many were jealous of her, and her star had risen rapidly, yet she seemed down to earth, didn't take drugs or get drunk, take off her clothes, or get into trouble. She seemed like a sweet (albeit very talented and pretty) girl next door.

But what most intrigued me about her, and made me stop to watch the concert, was the legendary fierce loyalty of her fans. Woe betide any journalist who said something negative about her—the enraged response of millions would be upon his or her head in a moment. I wanted to know why.

Within minutes I had her secret. Her first words were *"Wow! I'm so glad to meet you! This is so exciting!"* She smiled sweetly and then began chatting to the huge audience as if it were a few people at a coffee bar with her, hanging out and talking about things young people talk about—heartbreak, hurt feelings, or self-doubt.

She seemed so normal and so relatable and so, so glad to be friends with me—uh, I mean—the people in the audience. She was nice but not sugary sweet—she had an edge.

At one point she talked about being hurt by the vicious criticism of a journalist who had written nasty things about her. It had devastated her, and she got her revenge by writing a song about it that won 2 Grammy awards. The rallying refrain of the song was *"Some day I'll be living in the big ol' city, but all you're ever gonna be is mean."* Her fans loved it. Every one of them who had been bullied or hurt by someone felt it was their song. It was revenge—sweet, satisfying revenge.

She talked about getting back at boyfriends who had dropped her for someone else. She wrote songs about them. Everyone related. They felt that Taylor seemed to understand.

Taylor Swift is a genius at gaining rapport.

Why Has Amanda Knox Been Convicted of Murder Twice in Italy?

Amanda Knox is another blonde American girl who moved to Perugia, Italy to study languages in 2007. She shared a house with several other students; one was an English girl named Meredith Kercher, who was found brutally murdered in her room one morning. Knox and her boyfriend were convicted of the murder despite there being no forensic evidence connecting them to the killing.

Italians are emotional and expressive; Knox showed no emotion during her trial. She did a somersault in the police station after being arrested, which was recorded on camera for the world to see. Her expressionless eyes and demeanor, plus other rather unusual behavior—in my opinion—were what got her convicted. Despite the trial being overturned and Amanda returning home to the States, the Italians retried her in absentia and convicted her again.

That conviction has since been overturned and she is now clear and free.

Amanda Knox broke rapport with the public early on after her arrest. She seemed utterly unaware of how she came across to others. I contend that had she shown some emotion—grief for the dead girl, or horror and fear at what she had been accused of—and acted the way people would expect someone in her situation to act, the results of the trial might have been different. Instead she appeared sullen and disengaged.

Amanda Knox has no rapport skills. She may well be innocent, but her lack of rapport ensured her conviction. Well, that's my take anyway.

What is Rapport?

The word *rapport* comes from the French word meaning connection or correspondence. It means to be in harmonious or sympathetic relation to someone. We are in rapport when we feel affinity, compatibility, or empathy with the person we are with. We feel on the same wavelength and that we understand each other.

Some people just ooze rapport and we call them charismatic. Charming. A delight to be around.

When we are in rapport with someone we feel comfortable and accepted; it's a relationship of trust. We may feel like we have known the other person for a long time, even though we have just met.

So what precisely causes this feeling of rapport? It's actually a feeling of familiarity—at the unconscious level we sense we are *like* the other person and this makes us comfortable. We pick up signals from their clothes, style, body language and manner of speaking that we identify with and that makes us feel we know them already.

People like people who are like them.

In NLP (Neuro-linguistic Programming), rapport is considered a skill and as such can be cultivated and learned.

Many famous entertainers have great rapport skills. Oprah has a way of making you feel like you know her, that you could sit down and have a chat with her despite her huge celebrity. She would *understand* you. She would be *interested* in what you have to say.

Politicians try hard to develop rapport skills, with varying success. One thing for sure, if one does manage to develop rapport, he or she will almost certainly win an election. Ronald Reagan was a master at it—he won by getting the votes of people who didn't agree with his policies but loved the way he talked. They felt at ease with him. He was always friendly and seemed to like people. Richard Nixon had no rapport skills, which contributed to his downfall. No one cared what happened to him, because he didn't relate to people.

Notice what happens when you are *naturally* in rapport with someone. When you are naturally in rapport your body language seems to mirror the other person—you sit in the same position, you make eye contact, and even your movements seem to be similar. In addition your voice tones will match and the speed at which you are speaking will be more or less the same.

Watch two people in a restaurant who are clearly getting along. Observe how their body language will match and mirror each other.

The First Step in Developing Rapport

So the first step if we want to *develop rapport deliberately* is to become aware of the body language of the other person and ease into similar positions and movements. We can match voice tone and speed, and even breath rate. Both of us will feel comfortable.

This is called 'matching and mirroring' and is not the same as mimicry or copycatting. If you match and mirror someone's body language, eye contact and voice tone, they will feel respected, listened to, and approved. And above all, they will feel comfortable with you. Isn't that a good thing?

Taylor Swift demonstrated the body language and voice of a good friend chatting to you. She was relaxed and easy, open and accessible. She *confided*.

And More Rapport

Another way you get in rapport with someone is by really listening, paying attention, and talking about what the other person is interested in. It's about finding areas of commonality and focusing on them. When we first meet people, we automatically begin gently searching for grounds of commonality—where are you from, what do you do, what are your interests? In other words, what can we chat about, and how are we alike?

Rapport helps your communication and ensures you are understood. It's not about being manipulative; it's about being *flexible*. Big difference. Being flexible is about meeting people where they are and not insisting they meet you where you are.

Get interested in people and you will always have rapport.

Sacred Cow Alert!

The Cow Says:
"People have to accept me as I am.
I'm not changing who I am for other people."

Well, um, sorry to say this, but people don't have to accept you and frequently they won't. This Cow is currently lying on your couch, hooves up, munching popcorn. It will take a lot to shift this old gal. But she needs to move on out to where she belongs.

Once again, on the surface, it's hard to argue with the logic of a Sacred Cow—surely we ARE OK as we are? Surely people

SHOULD accept us—warts and all? Surely we shouldn't change our behavior just because someone gets upset with us?

Sure. All that's true. But it isn't always useful or the most pragmatic choice. The shadow side of this cow is the opinionated, strong minded, argumentative rebel. These types don't need to stick to their guns no matter what—they need to put them down and make a peace offering.

In other words, some of us need to flex our behavior so that it fits in better with other people. We need to be more sensitive, not less, in order to get along. Many of us need to change our behavior because it's not working.

"For things to change, I need to change."

Jim Rohn

Remember, getting along with people is a *skill* and as such is a learned behavior and can always be improved. We are not all born with these skills. It would be great if we all could accept each other as we are. But unfortunately, that isn't always the case.

And no, sometimes we're NOT OK as we are.

- *It's not OK* if **you fight or argue a lot** and are upsetting your friends.

- *It's not OK* if **you're lonely** because you can't keep your friendships going.

- *It's not OK* if you are **always being misunderstood** because your communication skills are lacking.

- And *it's not OK* if you're **wasting a lot of psychic energy** trying to put out fires for which you are responsible, or trying to soothe feelings you have hurt.

Of course, you have to balance a willingness to flex and change with consistency and congruency in your behavior. The secret is to balance consistency with flexibility; *be you* and also *be willing to adapt and change* where necessary.

Choose Nice

"When the choice is to be right or to be kind, always make the choice that brings peace."

Wayne Dyer

We all want choices. Choices give us freedom. We want to stay young at heart and flexible and able to influence those around us in positive ways. We want people to understand the intention of our communication.

Most of all, we want an easy life. Peace. Unruffled feathers.

This book encourages you to take 100% responsibility for your life, your behavior, and your results. It teases you away from being the Victim or from placing blame for your results on anything or anyone outside yourself. Only when you are totally responsible, and at cause, can you begin to create the results you want in life.

Isn't Deliberately Cultivating Rapport Manipulative?

Good question. And the answer is no. Or rather, it doesn't have to be.

Don't confuse manipulative, with useful and pragmatic. All sales training, marketing, relationship advice, religious teachings, and public relations, is potentially manipulative. We're not talking Scientology here. We're talking about skills you can learn to help you get along with people. Everybody wins. Manipulation is all about the motive.

If cultivating rapport sounds strange to you, think about when you have been *out of rapport* with someone and how awkward it feels. For instance, have you ever experienced a time when you have been upset about something and a friend was trying to calm you down? And it may have made you feel more upset because the other person didn't seem to 'get' what you were upset about. And somehow because they were calm and you weren't, you felt in the wrong.

There may have been a time when you were disturbed about something and went to a friend to let off steam, only to have them tell you to *relax* and that you are being overly dramatic? How did that make you feel? Worse than before, I imagine. You probably felt misunderstood, and worse, *judged.*

Instead, if your friend says something like, *wow, that must be awful!* You immediately feel better. Someone understands!

To get into rapport with someone who is upset, all you need to do is simply match and acknowledge their stress for a minute or two, and then gradually bring it down to a calmer tone. They will feel understood and will be happy to follow your lead. If you match their mood, it immediately deflates the emotional charge.

Trying to calm an upset person with soothing words, or worse, trying to talk them out of it, invariably has the opposite effect.

You defuse an upset person by showing them you *understand* them first. This is what gaining rapport is all about.

Can You Get Into Rapport With Strangers?

Yes you can! If you match mood, voice tone, and manner of speaking, anyone you come in contact with will feel more comfortable with you. I *guarantee* you this works.

Caveat: It doesn't mean you have to be rude if they are, but if someone speaks softly, then match it; if they speak excitedly, then match it; friendly, match it. You will find your transactions go more smoothly. Everyone wins.

In the case of aggression or rudeness, it *never* helps to act submissive or apologetic. So match their voice tone and manner at a slightly lower level using non-aggressive words. I urge you to try this and be amazed at what happens.

If your interactions with people go more smoothly, you will be more at peace. How much time and energy do we waste on unsuccessful interactions where we felt misunderstood and someone got upset as a result? I know for me an unpleasant interaction can color my whole day if I let it. Who needs that?

Rapport skills: Adopt this. It will make your life easier and everyone happier.

Personality Styles

There are even deeper levels to rapport. We all know people who we really like and are able to communicate with easily; others seem as if they are from another planet.

One reason we seem to 'click' with some people and not others may be because of personality styles. Everyone has a basic personality style with a mix of several others. It can be very useful to look at the **four basic personality styles** and learn how they interact with each other. It may provide you with a clue as to why you get along better with some people than with others.

The model I'm about to show you is for the purpose of *understanding* yourself and others—it's not about labeling you or putting anyone in a box. We have four basic personality styles and each of us is a combination of several, and usually one is dominant. There is no test to box you in—you choose which ones resonate with you. There is no score, no right or wrong answers.

The styles are as follows:

Pragmatic

The Pragmatic is direct, practical, punctual, no-nonsense and doesn't like to beat around the bush—a direct communicator. Results oriented, competitive, likes to lead, the Pragmatic doesn't suffer fools gladly and is a quick decision maker. Not especially good at rapport and doesn't care. Impatient by nature, can be rude, but sensible, gets things done. The Pragmatic is driven by the question
—Is this useful?
Ex. Steve Jobs

Socializer

The Socializer is open, direct and confident. Wants to be liked and wants to like you. The Socializer is friendly, people oriented, and craves excitement and challenge. Direct communicators. Great rapport skills. Bored easily, the Socializer is driven by the question
—Is this fun?
Ex. Bill Clinton

Amiable

Amiables want everyone to be happy and above all need to feel they can trust you. They tend to be patient and caring, good listeners and slow decision makers. Laid back. They dislike pushy people, arguments and fighting, and want to take time to get to know you. They are predictable, indirect, and dislike too much change or risk taking. Good rapport skills. The Amiable is driven by the question

—**Do I feel comfortable with this?**

Ex. Ronald Reagan

Analytic

Analytics are serious, logical, rational, and detail oriented. They like facts and figures and need lots of personal space. They will want to know your credentials if working with you. Indirect communicators. They are precise, task oriented and slow decision makers. Usually low on rapport skills. They won't be rushed into anything. They are unimpressed by enthusiasm and emotion and are driven by the question

—**Do I have enough information?**

Ex. Bill Gates

The Pragmatic will intimidate the Amiable and the Amiable might annoy and exasperate the Pragmatic.

The Socializer may seem flakey and shallow to the Analytic, and the Analytic will seem boring and fussy to the Socializer.

My profile is that I am primarily a Pragmatic with Socializer tendencies. I need excitement and challenge or I get bored; I like to be with people and am primarily interested in how they work. I'm friendly, outgoing and sociable and I tend to gloss over detail in favor of the big picture. Don't bore me with detail! Get to the point! I can be impatient and too direct at times. I'm also Aries.

It's the Pragmatic part of me that gets me into trouble. Too direct, too honest, wanting to get things done. Scary sometimes.

I share very little with the Analytic and to a lesser extent the Relater. Therefore those are the styles I need to make the most effort with in order to get along. For instance, if I am with an Analytic, I need to remember to be more serious, back off and not be pushy. I need to quiet down and avoid too much excitement or emotion. If I am with an Amiable I need to be less direct and gentler in my manner so that I don't intimidate. Amiables tend to be terrified of Pragmatic types.

Analytics need to lighten up; Pragmatics need to soften up; Socializers need to get serious; and Amiables need to develop a thicker skin. Each type has its strengths and weaknesses.

If you can recognize your own style and the styles of the people you are around, you can choose to flex your style and get into rapport with everyone. *This is a powerful tool for getting along with people.* All people, all the time. Notice the styles of your friends and intimates. Are you the same or different? Can you use this in order to make your relationships smoother? Does this explain why some people are so easy for you to relate to and others not so much?

I urge you to

- *Jump in and use it straight away* if you are Pragmatic because you will find it works

- *Play with it* if you are a Socializer—you'll have fun

- *Try it out cautiously* if an Amiable because it will help you get along with everybody

- *Examine it studiously* for its efficacy if an Analytic!

The Law of Requisite Variety

The Law of Requisite Variety is a fancy term in Neuro-Linguistic Programming that holds a simple truth. The law comes from the field of cybernetics and states that *the part of a system that holds the most flexibility holds the most influence in that system.*

The most flexible part is the strongest; therefore the person who has the most choices of behavior in any given situation, will have the most influence, be the strongest, and have the most success.

Applying these concepts to you and me works like this—when we have more choices and flexibility we are able to manage a situation better than someone who is rigid and limited.

When we age we tend to become rigid and inflexible and unable to adapt to changing circumstances. We stay young as long as we are flexible.

This book has been about giving you choices in your behavior. We need variety and options in techniques, styles and strategies in order to get along with everyone all the time. We are going to have to *be flexible* to get the results we want.

You now have more options: you can choose to get into rapport with someone; you can choose to be in control of your emotions and hurt feelings; you can choose to forgive and forget; you can choose to change the way you communicate with people if you're not getting along with them. The list of choices is endless once *you decide it's OK to be flexible and are willing to make the changes you need to make.*

Review

So **Skill #4** is to tune into rapport and learn how to make everyone feel right at home with you. Becoming aware of body language and personality styles will enable your relationships to improve with everyone. It's all about awareness and being willing to make the effort to be friendly and charming. It makes life so much easier!

Now let's move on to the next secret—**Skill #5.** This next Skill ties right in with rapport. In fact, it underlies all rapport skills. Can you guess? It's the secret to playing nice, but it's more than being nice.

Have you ever wondered if anyone would come to your funeral? They will come in droves if you adopt this next habit—you'll be genuinely missed.

Skill #5
Make Friendship and Unity Your Number One Priority

"We're ONE, but we're not the same. We get to carry each other, carry each other..."—U2

"As I've watched those who are deeply loved, I've noticed they all regard people as a basic source of happiness. Their companions are very important to them, and no matter how busy their schedules, they have developed a lifestyle and a way of dispensing their time that allows them to have several profound relationships."

Alan Loy McGinnis—*The Friendship Factor*

People who get along with people do so because they value them. They value all their relationships and give them priority. If you make friendship and unity your top value then it will become easy to get along with everybody all the time.

This means making sure your friends and relationships matter more than being right all the time and more than holding on to your sensitive feelings. When we can learn to consider our friends to be as important as our closest and most beloved family members, then we are on the road to getting along with them all the time.

My Mother

My mother got along with everybody all the time. She was kind and easy going and she always seemed overwhelmed with gratitude when someone wanted to be her friend. She never turned anyone down. A classic Amiable in personality.

My sisters and I used to worry about her, as she got older. We would grill her about who she had let in her apartment—sometimes we would not approve—but she always ignored us. If someone wanted her friendship, she would give it unstintingly. Now many of you may think this is silly, because people take advantage of people who don't discriminate, and it's also true that many people are boring or unpleasant to have around. I can relate to that thinking, but my mom wasn't like that.

My mom never had an enemy and never 'fell out' with anyone. Ever. She never had harsh words for people or lost her temper. She never gossiped and if she heard unkind words being said about someone, it seemed to hurt her, not them.

When she died at age 93, many people seemed genuinely moved because she was always so kind to everyone.

I would love to be like my mother. But I'm not. I'm impatient, have strong emotions and opinions. I can get mad easily. I can be stubborn. I was the baby in the family, with two older sisters. Although they deny it, they used to tease me, make me angry, and torment me. It was just so tempting to wind me up and get me going and I was such an easy target. They could easily get me to start screaming with anger and I'm sure it was great entertainment. My parents didn't do much about it; I was the youngest and the older two seemed to be turning out OK. I think they found me amusing and figured I'd learn what I needed to when I needed to.

It took me well into my adulthood to learn what I needed to: the skills to having great relationships. One influential 'aha' moment was Brian Tracy's admission that he used to be obnoxious and argumentative (me too Brian!) and yet he was able to change his behavior and be popular with everyone. Another was recognizing the secret my mom held—value any and all friendships.

This is one of the secrets that changed everything; place friendship and unity above everything else. When I really got that (and it took me awhile), everything started changing for me.

My mantra now is—*Friendship and unity first. Nothing matters more than unity. I will let go of being right or pushing my point of view. I will just drop whatever is causing disunity. It's not worth it.*

Hang On a Minute!

But wait! I hear you cry! Shouldn't we discriminate as to whom we have around us? Don't all the personal development teachers and psychologists tell us that having negative people around us can spoil our peace? Aren't we supposed to be careful regarding the company we keep?

Surely, saying anyone and everyone can be our friend is naïve and dangerous!

Sacred Cow Alert!

The Cow says:
"Get rid of all the negative people in your life. Say good bye to all toxic relationships!"

This Cow is so sacred she comes garlanded with flowers around her neck and alfalfa in her mouth. She is quoted everywhere and has been embraced with alacrity by almost every personal development guru, psychologist, therapist, and talk show host in vogue. Every one of them admonishes that negative people in your life will sabotage your success, hold you back, and undermine your self-confidence and happiness.

On Facebook the other morning I saw this post:

"Evaluate the people in your life! Then promote, demote, or terminate. You are the CEO of your life!"

Tony A. Gaskins Jr.

It had hundreds of 'Likes'. The comments were universally positive. I literally cringed when I read it. It struck me as arrogant and intolerant.

Or how about this one:

"Stop inviting people who don't celebrate you to your party! It's YOUR life—you have the right to be exclusive."

Mandy Hale—*The Single Woman: Life, Love, and a Dash of Sass*

On the surface, these bits of new age wisdom appear sound.

- Take control!

- Put yourself first for a change!

- Because you're worth it!

- You deserve to be happy!

- Stop letting other people dictate your agenda for life!

- If people don't support you 100%, don't invite them to your party of life!

This, and similar advice, usually using the words 'toxic', 'energy vampire' or 'unconscious' to describe people who you don't like having around, is so all pervasive that I don't think anyone ever questions how pernicious it can be.

Like all Sacred Cows it has its truth. I'm not denying it has helped many people.

If you are in an abusive relationship, either emotionally or physically, you need to get out—quickly. If your partner is an alcoholic or drug addict who refuses to acknowledge the condition and refuses to get help—get out. Don't negotiate, don't try to change the other person, don't wait around—get out before you are sucked into the vortex that abuse, alcohol and drugs will draw you into. It will destroy your health, happiness and finances. It could kill you.

And, sad to say, if you are involved with someone who is mentally ill, and this person refuses to get help, you may need to get him or her out of your life. You can rarely help people who are mentally ill if you are not qualified to do so, and they can destroy you with their illness.

Many people tolerate intolerable situations because they lack the courage or self-esteem needed to get out. The advice to take control and leave immediately can literally save lives.

A Mean Mother

I have a friend, Anna, whose mother is simply mean. She has emotionally abused Anna her whole life and continues to do so even though Anna is now in her 60s. She criticizes her every decision, makes negative comments on her hair and makeup and bullies her with threats about her inheritance. With the help of a psychologist, and a course in non-violent communication, Anna has learned to stand up to her mother for the first time, and control her mother's access to her life. She has learned how to use assertive language and no longer keeps her mouth shut when insulted. This has been liberating and life-enhancing for Anna.

This is positive and I applaud the use of the Sacred Cow in these circumstances.

What I object to and cringe over is the cavalier way this cow has been embraced by people who are too lazy to try and get things to work. Relationships are hard. They require effort and attention. Good ones don't just 'happen'.

My First Coach in San Miguel

The story of my first coach in San Miguel demonstrates both sides of this lesson.

When I was with my (now) husband before we were married, I was seeing a life coach/psychologist to help me through the transition period I was in. I had moved from my beloved England to Mexico. My kids had grown up and left home, I was divorced and trying to start a new life in San Miguel de Allende, Mexico with my new 'novio' Luis.

This relationship was a cultural shock for both of us. Although Luis was well traveled and a man of the world, he was still a strong-minded Mexican male at heart and had never come up against a female force like me.

I am a Woodstock Generation Boomer, an old hippie at heart—a liberated American female with a strong personality. Whew. The inevitable conflagration occurred periodically between us as we attempted to make sense of the other. He frequently felt I was trying to boss him around, and I in turn sometimes felt he was trying to control me. Fireworks.

Enter my coach/psychologist into the mix. She was someone I felt I could talk to about my feelings and sort through what was happening to me. I unloaded my frustrations on her.

"Get rid of him," she advised. *"You don't need this. You're just staying with him for security."*

"But wait, I like him!" I protested. *"He's wonderful when we're not fighting. We have so much in common—I just need to learn how to handle him. He's not like anyone I've met before. And he's not unkind, just different."*

"You're a coward. Afraid to look after yourself and be on your own. Get rid of him and stop using him as a security blanket!" She sternly admonished.

Fortunately I didn't heed her advice. I began to wonder who was really the bully or toxic person in my life. I decided it was she, not Luis. It was the best decision I ever made, to drop her as my coach.

Luis and I have been happily married now for 7 years and enjoy our differences. Life is never boring! It took some effort, but has definitely been worth it. We have a great life, traveling a lot, seeing relatives often, and enjoying the rest of our time in sundrenched, bougainvillea-draped Mexico. We have many friends and productive activities. Yes, well worth the effort we both put in to get it to work.

The irony is I had to let my coach go out of my life while she was advising me to get rid of someone else. So I used her advice—against her. I gave my relationship with her a lot of energy but decided in the end she was not a good influence on me.

I have since learned that my erstwhile coach has tried to destroy other relationships in town. She clearly doesn't believe that any uncomfortable situation should be tolerated. If it's not perfect, ditch it, is her philosophy. It almost seems as if she is jealous when she sees others in a relationship.

Was she right that I was looking for security? Probably. Who isn't? There is nothing wrong *per se* with wanting security. It's nice. And it's not as if that was the whole story or the only thing I was looking for.

She embraces the Sacred Cow of getting rid of toxic people in your life. Problem is, she takes this great teaching out of context and uses it as an excuse to be lazy. There is no room here for forgiveness, for letting things go, for being tolerant of others' shortcomings, or for taking the beam out of your own eye first.

She is utterly alone, by the way, with three ex-husbands and children who won't speak to her.

Never take relationship advice from someone who doesn't have good relationships!

"If you meet someone whose soul is not aligned with yours, send them love and move along."

Wayne Dyer

Corral This Cow

So let's corral this Sacred Cow of getting rid of all negative people in your life and hang a big bell around her neck so we know when she's coming. She's a wise old girl but can be easily misused by people who just don't want to make the effort involved in getting relationships to work.

There is a wonderful legend about the Buddha. The legend goes that he kept a cranky, negative, constantly complaining monk near him all the time. When he was questioned as to why he kept this toxic old man who criticized the Buddha's every move, so close to hand, the Buddha replied, *"Oh, because he's my best teacher!"*

So, like the Buddha, (who is a better example to follow than a New Age guru or television talk show host) why not start to regard annoying people as your teachers, helping you to evolve and develop? Difficult people can assist us to take charge of our emotions and responses. They can teach us how to control our negative reactions and take responsibility for what happens in our lives.

The Buddha constantly evaluated what his cantankerous sidekick was saying about him. He knew not to take it personally. Yet he noticed how he was eliciting those responses in the old fellow, honed his behavior, and became more flexible as a result of being around him.

I'm not saying we can all be like the Buddha. But how much better would it be to try and learn from negative people how we can improve, become more detached, and change what we need to change? How much will we miss if we just throw people away when they don't please us, as if they were disposable commodities?

What I'm advocating is that we give people a chance when they make mistakes or make us unhappy. Nobody's perfect and you can misinterpret people and make wrong assumptions about them. Give someone the benefit of the doubt and try to make things work before you pull the plug on a friendship.

You Can Pull the Plug Gently

Eckhart Tolle says,

> *"At times you may have to take practical steps to protect yourself from deeply unconscious people. This you can do without making them into enemies."*

I love this remark. There is no need to make enemies of people. Just quietly get on with your life. If they are deeply unconscious, just avoid them.

The Indian teacher Jiddu Krishnamurti used to say that there was no reason to end things violently, i.e. with pronouncements, confrontation or conflict. Just become aware and conscious and let it go without drama. It will die of its own accord.

> *"The self-help industry seems capable of cranking out an endless supply of books, tapes, and seminars that advocate believing in yourself, tapping the unlimited power within yourself, asserting yourself, competing confidently, taking advantage of the other person before the other person takes advantage of you, and telling anyone who does not give you what you want to get lost...*
>
> *But my experience in counseling such people is that when they push others away, intimidate their competitors, and disregard those to whom they have responsibility, they get to the front of the line and discover that there is no one there hand them any prizes."*

Alan Loy McGinnis—*The Friendship Factor*

Forgiveness

"Forgive everybody, all the time, for everything."

Brian Tracy

This was another gem from Brian Tracy. Just let it go. Whatever it is. It's not worth making a fuss. That way you will be free of drama and have great relationships. Is this difficult to do? Yes and no. If you make it your default mode then it gets easier.

Forgiveness could be considered a selfish act because it is so liberating and brings such peace. So if you must, do it for yourself and not for others. Whatever your motives, everyone wins when you practice forgiveness. Just decide ahead of time you are not going to put energy into being upset with someone. It's not the same as condoning something bad someone did.

I know I have stated several times that this book is not about abusive relationships and it's not. But it is true that people who have been victims of violence or abuse, *once they have spoken out and demanded justice*, report that when they let go and just drop it, i.e. forgive, they feel a tremendous sense of release and relief.

Ho'oponopono—a True Miracle?

Ho'oponopono is an ancient Hawaiian technique of mental cleansing. In the old days it involved family and village conferences where confession, repentance and forgiveness were established after much discussion, soul searching, and prayer.

The idea behind it is that when there is disharmony or trouble among individuals in a family or village, *everyone* is somehow responsible for creating the disharmony. Therefore everyone has to join in the reconciliation, accept their role in creating the problem, forgive themselves and each other and release it.

The technique and philosophy behind it have been incorporated into a modern method of healing and reconciliation for individuals.

Dr. Joe Vitale, writer and self-help guru, tells an amazing story about how he discovered this ancient Hawaiian technique of reconciliation:

> *"Two years ago, I heard about a therapist in Hawaii who cured a complete ward of criminally insane patients-- without ever seeing any of them. The psychologist would study an inmate's chart and then look within himself to see how he created that person's illness. As he improved himself, the patient improved. When I first heard this story, I thought it was an urban legend. How could anyone heal anyone else by healing himself? How could even the best self-improvement master cure the criminally insane? It didn't make any sense.*
>
> *The Hawaiian therapist who healed those mentally ill people would teach me an advanced new perspective about total responsibility. His name is **Dr. Ihaleakala Hew Len**...he worked at Hawaii State Hospital for four years. That ward where they kept the criminally insane was dangerous..."*

Joe Vitale contacted the doctor and spoke to him. Dr. Len told him that he never saw his patients face to face. He would sit in his office and review their files. Then, he would work on himself. And as he worked on himself, patients began to heal.

After a few months, shackled patients were allowed to walk free and previously hopeless inmates were released. In time, the ward emptied and was closed.

Dr. Len claimed that he was simply healing the part of himself that created the illnesses. He explained that total responsibility for your life means that everything that shows up in your life is at some level, (and frequently inexplicably), your responsibility. When we heal that part of us that created the illness or unhappiness, we heal others too.

This amazing story is true and Dr. Len and Joe Vitale have written a book called *Zero Limits* that fleshes out the technique of Ho'oponopono. You can find it at www.amazon.com/Zero-Limits-Secret-Hawaiian-System/dp/0470402563.

In a nutshell, the technique employs four phrases:

- Please forgive me

- I'm so sorry

- I love you

- Thank you.

These phrases are to be repeated over and over while thinking about the afflicted person or the person you are having problems with. You focus on them initially and then you focus on healing that part of you that caused the problem. It's that simple.

Review

So **Skill #5** is to make friendship your highest priority. It will serve you well. When you absolutely have to let go of people because they are harming you in some way, you can do it with compassion and awareness. There is never a need for drama and conflict. And always in the first instance give people and relationships the benefit of the doubt and a second chance.

We have one more skill to go. Each skill is as important as the others and this next one is no exception. This one will guarantee an easier, more peaceful life. If you put the next one into practice then you will definitely live a calmer existence with no more embarrassing scenes, regrets, sleepless nights or disappointment with your own behavior. Have you guessed it? All you have to do is...

Skill #6
Drop the Drama!

Story time!

"You want peace. There is no one who does not want peace. Yet there is something else in you that wants the drama, wants the conflict...."

Eckhart Tolle—*A New Earth*

"That's it! I'm done! We're finished! I can't believe I've been so blind and stupid!"

My friend Gabrielle was obviously upset.

"What in the world happened?" I asked, getting curious.

"It's Miguel. I am so totally over him. I don't care if I never see him again after what he did. I've had a close call. I suppose I'm lucky to have seen the light. What happened is gross beyond measure."

Miguel was Gabrielle's erstwhile boyfriend—she is American, he Mexican. They are both in their 60s. They had been seeing each other on and off for several years, and it had been winding down

85

for most of that time. Her friends were somewhat exasperated with them both and tired of the relationship.

"OK, shoot. What's going on? I'm listening." My imagination now in overdrive—I was quite sure she must have caught him trying to steal something, by the sound of horror in her voice.

"Pickled pig's feet, that's what!"

Huh?

"We had an arrangement", she explained. *"He was supposed to bring over a meal for our last night together before I go back to the States. He brought pickled pig's feet!*

Have you ever heard of anything so disgusting? Who does he think I am? Who does that? He obviously has no respect for me and this is too gross for words. He even had the nerve to offer me some!"

I was speechless for a moment and then offered some mangled words of comfort. I decided not to volunteer that for many Mexicans pickled pig's feet are a delicacy. It wouldn't have gone down well. I carefully hid my amusement.

The truth is I didn't want to challenge her version of events. It made a great story she could tell her friends back in the States when they asked how she and Miguel were doing. It hid the sad and boring truth, which was that the relationship was dead in the water and had been for some time.

When they had met, Miguel had been a handsome Mexican accountant, educated and charming. He didn't speak English, or she much Spanish, but in the early days the language difficulties didn't matter. The sparks flew and they were in love. She could see a future with him in beautiful San Miguel de Allende, her adopted home. What fun! She was proud to be seen with him and enjoyed telling her friends back home in the States about her handsome Mexican boyfriend.

Somewhat disconcertingly, Miguel didn't actually have a job in accounting. In fact, he had no job at all, and although educated, he seemed to lack ambition. He drank too much and eventually stopped being a lot of fun. He never paid for their meals out. The relationship rather quickly took a downward turn, and for several years had ben running on empty, a sad reminder of the early heady days.

Pickled pig's feet made a great story to tell friends. Much better than the mundane reality, which was vaguely embarrassing.

Drama! Gabrielle had unknowingly created this drama in order to get out of a mess she was wallowing in. If he liked that kind of food, *he had to go*. If he didn't have respect for her sensitivities, *he had to go*. If the cultural differences were so great, *he had to go*. Not the truth, which was that she now wanted out of the relationship and didn't know how to extricate herself gracefully.

Drama always has a hidden agenda. It is never what it seems. We create drama because we need it to hide behind and it is frequently easier than facing the truth. We create drama every day, all the time. Sometimes it helps us, but mostly it does not.

Drama can spoil friendships, exhaust partners, and use up huge amounts of psychic energy to keep it going. We can lose jobs over it and it can make our lives very uncomfortable if we are not careful.

Drama? Drop it! Don't create it and don't perpetuate it in others.

What Exactly is Drama?

What do I mean by drama? Drama is used in this context to mean the stories we make up about people and events in our lives in order to understand and give meaning to what is going on around us.

- Drama is when we **hallucinate what other people are thinking** and imagine the worst.

- Drama is when **we overreact** and get our feelings hurt over something somebody said or did. We sometimes call this *melodrama*.

- Drama is when we **continually find things to complain about** and make a big deal about them.

- Drama is **making a mountain out of a molehill**. Blowing up something out of proportion in order to get attention.

- Drama is the stories we make up about ourselves and the world around us.

Why Do We Create Drama?

We create drama to cover up hidden and unconscious agendas. We usually don't even know we are doing it.

We create drama to get out of doing something or to get out of a relationship. If we start a fight with someone we don't have to stick to our commitment with them.

We create drama to get attention. It works, but not the kind of attention we want.

Worst of all, we cling to our drama, and find ways to justify it and prove it true. This makes it difficult to forgive and forget—the very essence of great relationships. Our drama becomes our story.

Drama is the secret enemy of great relationships; it can destroy your peace of mind and the peace of mind of everyone around you.

The Stories We Tell

We are the only animals who create drama. Making up stories is enormously important to us—in fact humans are obsessed with it.

All fiction literature, theater, movies, TV, reality TV is drama, the fruit of someone's imagination.

The stories we tell give meaning to life and help us to make sense of our existence. Stories and myth help us cope with death and the fleetingness of everything in our lives. They allow us to escape from our own reality and enter into another.

Ancient myths, stories, and legends are empowering in that they help us make sense of the universe. They can be positive in impact.

But when it comes to the stories we tell about ourselves and negative drama we make up about circumstances and people—then we are dealing with something entirely different. Let's look at some of the forms of drama we indulge in.

Walking On Eggshells—Touchiness

There is nothing more frustrating than when someone takes what you say the wrong way. Maybe you have friends who do this. Whatever you say, you never know when they will get hurt feelings or take offense. You feel like you are walking on eggshells around them.

Touchiness is hard on everyone, but especially your friends. Touchiness is when we are overly sensitive and have a tendency to spin things in a negative way. We impute unkind motives to what someone said. It's all about ego—we are insecure and our ego wants attention and ratification.

Its first cousin is prickliness. Prickliness is being bad tempered or irritable.

I Have Issues!

"Nobody is paying attention to me!" cried my friend Jenna.

"What do you mean exactly" we asked, intrigued. We were four friends, having lunch together in one of the lovely sidewalk cafes

in San Miguel. We hadn't been together for a long while and had been chattering away excitedly, catching up.

"Well, when we are talking, nobody looks at me or listens to me. You all talk over me and drown me out. I was neglected as a child, so I have issues around this. It's not fair. You all know this. I'm leaving." She got up out of her chair.

"But we were all just chatting and yakking and we were drowning each other out. Nobody was singled out for this!" I insisted.

But she didn't hear me. As far as she was concerned, her friends didn't respect her, listen to her, or acknowledge her existence. We clearly didn't care about HER. It had been going on all her life.

Jenna felt she needed to create some drama around this 'issue' to get our attention and to validate that she counted. We of course were willing to do so because we loved her and we all understood that this was her modus operandi.

We soothed her ruffled feathers and made her sit down again. We listened to her, looked at her, paid attention to her. She was soon happy again; it had cast a slight pall but we were soon clucking away like hens again.

What was going on here? What went wrong? We all felt we were paying attention to each other, but Jenna's mind had created an entirely different reality, one that confirmed that she was unworthy and had never really been loved. Her 'Model of the World' meant she was predisposed to see hurt where it didn't exist and to project illusory intentions onto her friends' behavior. This caused her to be touchy sometimes and to create drama.

Ok, I'm feeling a…

Sacred Cow Alert!

The Cow says:
"I can't help being this way! I have issues!
It's all because of stuff that happened in my
childhood. Other people need to respect this!"

Well, no they don't and they won't. Now I know that some people have experienced very traumatic events in childhood and my heart goes out to them. But this Cow has become an excuse to create drama.

(This book is not about serious abuse. We are dealing with fairly normal childhood challenges).

Sometimes you have to just get over yourself. Most people who are of a certain age, (including old hippies!), have gone over their stories umpteen thousand times and are very familiar with all the ins and outs. We get very good at our stories, we repeat them and anchor them quite firmly until they become part of our identity.

Mainstream psychologists, TV show doctors, and I'm sorry to say some alternative therapists, encourage the re-enactment of traumatic incidences with the hope of purging them from the system. Unfortunately, it usually has the opposite effect.

Now I'm not saying that Jenna should have kept her mouth shut and repressed her feelings. But there are other ways to express how we are feeling without making everyone feel awkward and guilty.

Jenna could have banged on the table and said *"Girls! Listen to me! I'm trying to talk and you're all so loud you can't hear me!"* Then laughed and said what she wanted to say. Then she could have added, *"I sometimes feel nobody listens to me, but I know you don't mean it"*, or something along those lines. We would have gotten the idea and she would have made her point, without awkwardness or hurt feelings.

Or she could have just dropped it. By far the better choice…but hard to make when we are immersed in our own emotions.

Touchiness. Creating drama to get attention. It's all about me and my stuff. Drop it. You can choose to. Everybody has issues—you're not the only one. It's just not necessary and there are better ways to express how you are feeling.

Jealousy

Jealousy is another demonstration of drama. It is the suspicion or fear of being replaced by a rival; it can come from envy of another person's advantages or success. It always springs from fear, comparison, and competition. Jealousy is an age-old emotion and we only need to look at stories from the early books of the Bible to find jealousy—Cain kills his brother Abel in a fit of jealousy, Joseph's jealous brothers sell him into slavery. Many murders can be linked back to jealousy.

Jealousy is the most pernicious of all the negative emotions and is the cause of cutthroat competition and ruined relationships. *A fit of jealousy, a jealous rage*; terms we use to describe jealousy. When someone is jealous, it's like a form of madness and it can be impossible to negotiate or reason with the person who is caught up in the emotion. People will do things that destroy their own lives because of it.

Jealousy can make you miserable. If you compare yourself to others, there will always be someone who is better than you in certain areas. If you are jealous of a rival in love or friendship, it is fear based—you can't think straight because you are terrified of losing the person you love, or want as your friend.

Jealousy is obviously disruptive to relationships. It can show up in families, in romantic partners, at work among colleagues, and with friends. If someone just doesn't seem to like you, it could be jealousy at the root. If someone at work tries to undermine you and prevent your success, it certainly is jealousy. If your partner is acting strange and grumpy it could be jealousy. And among friends, if someone never says anything nice to you, it may be because they suffer from envy and just can't bring themselves to compliment you.

Jealousy has hidden agendas.

Jealousy leads to gossip and criticism. It is drama in a very destructive form. Drop it. Find ways to stop yourself from acting on it. It never helps to indulge it.

Certain alternative forms of therapy can be very helpful in overcoming jealousy—Emotional Freedom Techniques (EFT), The Sedona Method (described later in this chapter), Hypnotherapy, Life Coaching, Re-parenting, Matrix Re-imprinting—are just a few of the techniques you may want to explore. They are easily found via Google or YouTube.

A Needless Breakup

"I have to cancel our meeting this week," Angela said. *"June and I aren't speaking. We had a terrible fight."*

Angela and June were two friends I knew in England. We three used to meet once a week for lunch and chat—we used to laughingly call ourselves the 'No Sex in the City' gals after the then current television series where four friends met regularly to talk about men and sex. Our conversations were less exciting and rather more prosaic, but we enjoyed them immensely.

"Oh no. What happened?" I gasped.

"I offered to look after June's dog while she went on her weekend retreat. The dog is fine but she is furious with me because I didn't walk her every day. I was so afraid of losing her if I took her out, so I just let her out in the garden. Honestly, it was only 3 days—there was no harm done. The dog isn't well trained and I was terrified she would get away from me. The dog is happy and safe. What is her problem?"

"Hmm. Let me talk to her." I was slightly shocked that this would cause a rift in a long-term friendship.

When I spoke to June she was livid.

"I asked her specifically to walk the dog at least twice a day. The dog is just learning how to 'go' outside and I wanted to keep the good habits going. She didn't even take her out once! Did she just not care what I asked? Did she not listen? She is so controlling! Has to do things her way or not at all. Now all the training is out the window and my dog is doing her 'business' everywhere. Honestly? I just don't even want to be around Angela anymore. I can't trust her. She has no respect."

Boom. A friendship of many years' standing, now heading down the drain. Our lovely and enjoyable weekly meetings, cancelled. What had happened? Each side had an argument and I could see both sides of the story.

It was clear to anyone involved that this could easily have been solved with some give and take, apologies, and some understanding on each side.

But could it?

What was really going on here? Were two friends of long-standing really falling out over a misunderstanding over a dog, which was after all, alive and well?

No. There was a hidden agenda behind this drama and it was this: June no longer wanted to honor a commitment she had made a few months back to Angela regarding living arrangements. She wanted out and didn't know how to break it to June without seeming like a flake. So instead she started a fight, which gave her a comparatively easy way out. In a strange way, this was easier than telling the truth.

I'm pretty sure June was unaware of her true motives in this drama.

The consequence of this unconscious action was the loss of a mutually beneficial friendship. Not to mention my regular lunch date.

This happens all the time. Arguments and fights and *drama* among friends and partners are seldom caused by what appears on the surface.

The Least Popular Type of Person—Can You Guess?

"The judgmental temperament never generates much affection."

Alan Loy McGinnis—*The Friendship Factor*

Judging others is drama. It will never make you popular and will drive friends away. People will be uncomfortable around you. They will figure that if you are judging someone else harshly, then you are probably thinking the same thing about them. It is the first cousin of gossip and criticism and is a poison that will spoil your happiness and all your relationships.

Judgmental people usually judge themselves harder than anyone. Their judgments are a mirror of how they feel about themselves. Many were criticized harshly as children and don't like themselves much. Although they are hard to be around, they deserve compassion and not judgment from us.

"Judge not, that ye be not judged."

Judgment. Drop it. Just don't do it. Just keep what you are thinking to yourself.

The Worst Form of Black Magic

"Looking at everyday human interactions, imagine how many times we cast spells on each other with our word. Over time this interaction has become the worst form of black magic, and we call it gossip. Gossip is black magic at its very worst because it is pure poison."

Don Miguel Ruiz—*The Four Agreements*

The worst form of drama is gossip. Gossip is when we make up stories or pass on information about other people that is negative and catty. We do it behind their backs because we wouldn't dare say it to their faces. Gossip is cowardly. It is mean. It is passing judgment on another person without that person being able to defend himself.

People who gossip are invariably insecure. They believe deep down that you won't be interested in them unless they have some juicy tidbits to pass onto you. They do it to feel better about themselves and to make a connection to the person they are gossiping with. It is creating drama.

The problem with gossip is it poisons the minds of everyone involved. When you have talked negatively about someone you then feel you have to justify your own nastiness by proving that what you have said is true. Gossip makes it harder to let go of the drama of the story you have told or to admit you may have been wrong.

All great religious leaders and spiritual masters abhor gossip, slander and backbiting. It is drama at its worst and the enemy of all relationships. Once you have stooped to gossip about someone, it is very hard to ever be that person's friend. You will always feel a little guilty, and almost inevitably the gossip will get back to them.

Never, ever gossip. Drop it. It is truly *'black magic at its very worst.'*

So How Do I Drop It? Easier Said Than Done!

Drama shows itself as touchiness, arguing, jealousy and gossip. We are being dramatic when we get our feelings hurt or blame others for our problems. Drama is all about ego, playing the victim—it is selfish and shows insecurity. When you blow things up out of proportion, take remarks people make out of context, and make everything that goes on in the world all about YOU, then you are indulging in drama.

How do you drop the drama?

Like this:

- When *you* get in an argument, feel jealous or offended, get your feelings hurt, stomp off in a huff, or are just generally not getting along with somebody because of some silly story…. STOP! *You* are creating the drama, so just drop it, now. You can figure out later who was right or wrong and where the touchiness came from. In the meantime, drop it. The universe doesn't revolve around you. Get over it.

- Now, when *someone else* is causing the drama…. STOP! Drop it now. You can figure out later how guilty they were, or what the hidden agenda is, but for now DON'T

PERPETUATE THE DRAMA. Don't give it oxygen—don't comment, argue, tell them how silly they are being, react angrily, or gossip about it to others. Just let it go. Whatever you feel like saying right now, it's almost 100% certain you are better off not saying it.

Drama thrives on attention, sympathy, and indignation. Don't enable it. It will die a death without the juice of somebody noticing. It dies through neglect, indifference or disregard.

So the first step is awareness. Be honest with yourself—brutally honest. Are you creating drama? Probably. Most of us do.

Could you just let this go? The answer is always yes.

Read this chapter several times so that you become familiar with the different forms drama takes. Catch yourself at it. Unless you're a saint, you're most likely indulging in one of its forms.

Catch yourself and drop it like a hot potato. You will see your social life start to improve *dramatically*.

Second, don't perpetuate drama by reacting to it. Let it go. Don't rise to the bait. When other people are being dramatic, just remember there is a hidden agenda; try and figure it out so you can gain some distance and understanding.

So just make sure YOU are not the toxic person by creating drama. You drop it and stop responding to the drama of those around you.

The Sedona Method

A really simple and effective technique for letting go of negative emotions and drama is the *Sedona Method*. It was developed by Hale Dwoskin in the 1980s and is based on the work of his mentor, Lester Levinson. In his book *The Sedona Method,* (available on www.amazon.com) Dwoskin instructs on how to release any emotion, belief, or behavior. The process is easy and you can do it anytime, anywhere. The basic method is as follows.

The Method:

Focus on an issue that you would like to feel better about. Ask:

- Would I like to change it?

- This feeling, X, could I allow myself to have that feeling as best I can?

(Allow yourself to feel whatever you are feeling in this moment about the issue or problem.)

- Could I allow myself to feel as X as I do?

(Embrace it fully.)

- Could I welcome that feeling and allow it to be present?

(By allowing the feeling rather than resisting it, you allow it to flow freely through you and thus assist its release.)

- Could I just let it go? Only to the extent that I am able to, now?

- Would I?

(Would I rather have this feeling, or would I rather be free?)
- When?

(You are free to make the decision any time you choose.)

Obviously there are no right or wrong answers, but what you are aiming for is *yes, yes,* and *now.* Keep asking and going around the loop until you can't remember what the problem was or feel the emotion anymore.

> *"During this process welcome your thoughts, your sensations, your feelings, and the stories that you tell yourself. Just allow them all to be here and know that everything is okay as it is."*

Hale Dwoskin—*The Sedona Method*

You may find if you're having trouble releasing something it's frequently because you're focusing on the wrong emotion. When this stuck feeling happens, ask:

What is at the core of this feeling?

Could I allow myself to dive into this feeling?

Just keep releasing on what comes up and you may find different emotions arise that you were unaware of before. Keep asking until you reach a point where you can go no deeper. When you find the genuine feeling you may have a lovely "aha!" moment where you will experience a sense of peace and calm.

Finally...

If *you* drop the drama, like magic the people around you will start to drop it too. You will notice your world improving...like the ice melting in *The Lion, The Witch and the Wardrobe.*

Let's move onto some final thoughts...

Final Thoughts

"Because we depend so much on the affection and approval of others, we are extremely vulnerable to how we are treated by them. Therefore a person who learns to get along with others is going to make a tremendous change for the better in the quality of life as a whole."

Mihaly Csikszentmihalyi—*Flow*

April in San Miguel

I am finishing this book in April, in my beloved San Miguel de Allende in the mountains of Mexico. Spring is apparent everywhere—the jacarandas are in full bloom and the bougainvillea is competing for most beautiful plant in the universe. The landscape is bursting with color and allergies are rampant.

My garden is a veritable bird sanctuary—today I count more than 10 different species of bird, including Oriole, Hummingbird (one nesting on our porch), Grackle, House Finch, Dove, Woodpecker, Bushtit, Wren, Great Kiskadee, Vermillion Flycatcher (a little stunner), and next door the Black-Crowned

Night-Herons are gathering, after a winter vacation somewhere exotic.

I love observing the birds and can watch them for ages. They don't always get along perfectly and that's fun. There are frequent flare-ups; the Grackles complain endlessly and can be bullies, the Kiskadee is always shouting about something, fussing at her babies. The Doves can be irritable with each other in courting season; the female tires of the constant attention of her suitor and will do her best to avoid him. They create a lot of scandal in the branches. The Herons spat occasionally and the offended bird will fly off in a huff to another tree to sulk for a while.

So they are not so different from us. They do have their moments of ruffled feathers. But, as Eckhart Tolle observed while watching some quarreling ducks, unlike us they get over it quickly. The duck will flap its wings fiercely for a few seconds, getting rid of the negative energy, and will soon be back alongside the enemy duck, swimming peacefully. So do the birds in my garden. The offended Heron waits a minute or two and then flies back to the scene of the crime; all is forgiven and forgotten.

Among the birds there is no drama, no gossip relayed, no stories made up and passed on that make it so hard to let go of the irritation. At least I don't think so. The birds simply live in the moment and let things go. They have disagreements and irritations, but they drop them quickly.

We are different, but we don't have to be. We can choose to be like the birds and just let our hurts, offenses and stories go. We can choose to drop them, or better yet, not make them up in the first place. We may have to make these choices 10 times a day, but we still have that choice.

This book is about giving you choices. It's NOT about changing your personality, or becoming a different person in order to get along with people. It's not about becoming sweet or always keeping quiet. It is about playing nice.

Drop This, Adopt This

Unless you are a saint, you are always going to have little upsets and experience negative emotions from time to time. It's what you do about them that counts.

Just like the birds, there are a few rules that have to be observed. You absolutely must:

- Drop being the **victim**

- Drop making **excuses**

- Drop **blaming** others for your relationship failures

- Drop the judgment, criticism and gossip

- Drop the **laziness** and unwillingness to change.

Then you must adopt these skills:

- Take 100% responsibility for what shows up in your life

- The meaning of your communication is the response you get

- You don't always have to speak your truth

- Practice rapport, the greatest communication skill

- Make unity and friendship your highest priority

- Drop the Drama!

So there it is. **6 Drama-Draining Social Skills** to great relationships for those of us who just want some peace and harmony in our lives.

The whole theme of this book is about taking charge of your life, learning how to control your actions (and your mouth), accepting responsibility for everything that happens to you, and learning to play nice. Especially when you don't feel like it and you believe you're not naturally nice! We know now that's not true. You are nice, you just don't always feel nice.

These skills work. I promise you. Each one, if practiced, will work miracles in your life. You may want to write them down and put them up around your environment to remind you of their wisdom. Some people put their favorite sayings in their wallet or purse so they see them whenever they use money.

The wonderful discovery will be, that as you work on your behavior and improve your social skills, you will become a nicer person automatically. You will start feeling patient, kinder, adaptable and compatible. You will start to see yourself as an easy-to-get-along-with person. That feels good.

Good luck! And please, keep on being a Pirate, a Rebel. Don't change that. You can still get along with everybody, all the time.

Just play nice. And drop the drama. That's all that counts. The world needs you to be who you are.

Did you like what you just read?

If so I would LOVE and APPRECIATE a nice review. Reviews help indie authors more than you can possibly imagine. I will even buy you lunch if you're ever in San Miguel de Allende, Mexico.

That's a promise—tacos on me.

Please go to the book page for *Drop the Drama!* on Amazon.com and click on 'reviews.' Thanks!

About Margaret Nash

 Margaret Nash spends her time as a self-help writer, life-coach, seminar leader, and dog owner in San Miguel de Allende, a lovely, artistic haven in the central mountains of Mexico.

She grew up in the Deep South—Alabama—in the 1960s, before making her way to England where she lived for several decades before moving to Mexico.

Her website and blog—www.margaretnashcoach.com—and her books, *Rebellious Aging, Drop the Drama! Artful Assertiveness Skills for Women,* and *The Retirement Rebel* (check them out on the following pages) along with her regular workshops, deal with the themes of aging well, surviving transitions, and finding your groove in your 50s, 60s, and beyond.

Margaret's tribe is made up of the rebel-hippie-free-spirit type who is facing major life changes and determined to age in the coolest way possible—courageously.

She has been practicing as a life-coach for 17 years and trained as a Master Practitioner/Life Coach in NLP (Neuro-linguistic Programming), Hypnotherapy, and Time-line Therapy.

www.margaretnashcoach.com

Artful
Assertiveness
Skills For Women

Margaret
Nash

Old Hippie At Heart Series

Attention Ladies of all ages, shapes, sizes, and personalities! Would you like to learn how to stand up for yourself, gain respect, and handle *every* situation with calm assurance and authority? Yes?

Then you need to read this book! It's time for **Assertiveness Boot Camp** and this book is your self-help Boot Camp Guide.

So pull on your fatigues, lace up your boots, and let's get to work! Welcome to *Artful Assertiveness Skills for Women*.

Here you will learn the basic rules of assertiveness:

- Learn how to say no, artfully and effectively without anyone getting upset.

- Define and protect your boundaries without anyone noticing.

- Project a calm, confident energy that will make the Dog Whisperer jealous.

- Shut down bullies and passive-aggressive, catty types with style and wit.

- Learn the body language that will ensure you are listened to and taken seriously. Avoid these 7 common mistakes.

- Practice the best way to complain about bad service.

- Discover how to keep yourself safe both physically and emotionally.

But it takes some work! You'll going to learn some awesome and artful responses that will just trip off your tongue the next time you are upset, ignored, or challenged.

You will also pick up some very useful body language tips that may save your bacon one day and learn the secret of how to exude an energy that makes people sit up, listen, and treat you with respect.

This self-help guide is fun, easy to read and will keep you entertained with real life stories to illustrate how assertiveness works, or doesn't work.

You'll get Boot Camp homework—phrases and sentences to practice—after every chapter. You can literally just copy down useful responses and use them verbatim.

It's different from other assertiveness training—it really emphasizes the artful bit— which means you always come across and natural, friendly and relaxed while still getting the respect you deserve.

Time to get busy; it will change your life forever!

This is the 4th book in the *Hippie at Heart Self-help Series* by Margaret Nash, Life-Coach, Business Trainer, NLP Master Practitioner, self-help writer, aging brat, hippie at heart...as she shares her years of experience with clients, family, friends, dogs and cats, honing her assertiveness skills. (OK, it didn't work with the cats.)

What people are saying about *Artful Assertiveness Skills for Women*:

"This book has so much valuable advice on modern life for the modern woman. You'll learn how to handle difficult people and stressful situations --without stress! Margaret Nash offers a refreshing perspective on women's issues in the workplace and in day-to-day interactions." SP Ericson

*"This is a timely book. The rise of the **MeToo** movement spawns stories indicating far too many women lack skills in assertiveness. Standing up in situations where power is the undercurrent is hard. This is an important book. Nash's chapter on creating boundaries and another on 'combat training' made this an especially good read. Buy this for you.... and your daughters."* Barbara Pagano

"I teach assertiveness skills in my business and LOVE this book! Margaret provides clear stories and solutions so that reader's assertiveness muscles will get bigger and bigger as they flex their healthy, compassionate, courageous power." Trina

"This book delivers ~ chapter after chapter after chapter ~ and percolates along with such an upbeat and companionable delivery that the reader cannot help but gain an infusion of the Artful Assertiveness Skills author Margaret Nash promises!"

"While she employs such yang training metaphors as "Boot Camp" and "Test Pilots," she does so in a manner that serves the yin value of relationship: attaining these aptitudes not for "power-over" ends, but in order to cultivate win-win accord. As this book is written with women in mind, this is most satisfactory in terms of Jungian Psychology, which teaches that a woman's animus, or masculine dimension, is there to serve her womanly nature." Mary Trainor-Brigham

"Up 'til now I have been the kind of woman who usually said 'yes' when I really meant 'no'! Reading Margaret Nash's book has encouraged me to be more authentic with my real feelings with a new courage to speak my truth without being abrasive.

Having been a 'nice girl' all of my life, I was a natural people pleaser and generally said what people wanted to hear.

I'm very encouraged after reading and practicing 'Artful Assertiveness Skills for Women' and I'm enjoying this newfound freedom ... my communication skills have become more forthright. I have used many of the suggestions in this book ... especially the one of asking questions like, 'now why would you say that?' or 'What do you mean by that comment?' A question seems to stop an aggressive person in their tracks and the dynamic quickly changes. So far, I've not offended any of my friends and have a much better relationship with my employee who thought she was boss! I highly recommend." Sabrina

"This book lays out a concise, easy plan or boot camp for improving daily interactions with every person you encounter. With lists of exact actions & dialogues to facilitate desired outcomes, I wasn't surprised the author has spent much of her career as a life coach. It doesn't

read like a self-help book, but more as an action plan to guide us toward results. Easy & interesting read. Wish I had access to this at age 20 instead of 50!" Krista Yarnell

"Bought book at the local library for my 25 year old daughter and she loved it! Never too early or late to start learning this stuff!" Joseph Toone

Hippie at Heart Self-Help Series

REBELLIOUS
Aging

A Self-Help Guide for the
Old Hippie at Heart

MARGARET NASH

This book contains some of the best life coaching tips and techniques for personal transformation available on the planet today—and they will help you age like a Rebel!

Are you an unconventional, fiercely independent old hippie at heart, determined to age in the best way possible, but facing major life changes such as **divorce, relocation, retirement, or empty nest?**

Have these changes thrown you for a loop? And are you starting to feel stuck, losing your enthusiasm and zest for life, and as if you're in a fog?

You need to read this book!

Take heart! We're all in the same boat. Aging can be fun! You just need to awaken your *Rebel* and learn to live adventurously. Again.

This motivational, life-coaching self-help guide is just for you and will help you survive those transitions, get back on track, and emerge from that deep dark foggy forest as a new and improved version of yourself.

How? I hear you cry?

In this entertaining, practical, *and with a touch of the mystical,* guide, you will learn:

- The #1 reason you feel stuck and what you can do about it

- How to identify your *Archetypes* and use them as guides

- Define once and for all the story you are telling yourself about growing old and how to *rewrite that script*!

- The recipe for the secret sauce to discover your purpose and create your dream life!

It will inspire, motivate, and encourage you to *keep on truckin'.*

"The opposite of courage isn't cowardice, it's conformity."
Jim Hightower

Check out what others are saying:

Join the author, Margaret Nash, Life-Coach, self-help writer, and NLP trainer with over 20 years' experience, on her Hero's Journey to re-find her mojo and forge a new path in life, after facing a number of daunting challenges all at once.

Every idea, method and process outlined in this book is one that helped her get back behind the wheel and motoring again.